CW01020345

The Dad Rock That Made Me a Woman

AMERICAN MUSIC SERIES

Jessica Hopper, Charles L. Hughes, and Hanif Abdurraqib, Series Editors

Recent Titles

Franz Nicolay, *Band People: Life and Work in Popular Music*

Tara López, *Chuco Punk: Sonic Insurgency in El Paso*

Alex Pappademas and Joan LeMay, *Quantum Criminals: Ramblers, Wild Gamblers, and Other Sole Survivors from the Songs of Steely Dan*

Bruce Adams, *You're with Stupid: kranky, Chicago, and the Reinvention of Indie Music*

Margo Price, *Maybe We'll Make It: A Memoir*

Francesca T. Royster, *Black Country Music: Listening for Revolutions*

Lynn Melnick, *I've Had to Think Up a Way to Survive: On Trauma, Persistence, and Dolly Parton*

Lance Scott Walker, *DJ Screw: A Life in Slow Revolution*

Eddie Huffman, *John Prine: In Spite of Himself*

David Cantwell, *The Running Kind: Listening to Merle Haggard*

Stephen Deusner, *Where the Devil Don't Stay: Traveling the South with the Drive-By Truckers*

Eric Harvey, *Who Got the Camera? A History of Rap and Reality*

Kristin Hersh, *Seeing Sideways: A Memoir of Music and Motherhood*

Hannah Ewens, *Fangirls: Scenes from Modern Music Culture*

Sasha Geffen, *Glitter Up the Dark: How Pop Music Broke the Binary*

Hanif Abdurraqib, *Go Ahead in the Rain: Notes to A Tribe Called Quest*

Peter Blackstock and David Menconi, Founding Editors

The Dad Rock That Made Me a Woman

Niko Stratis

UNIVERSITY OF TEXAS PRESS AUSTIN

Pseudonyms have been used for some of the individuals discussed in the text.

Printed in the United States of America
First edition, 2025

∞ The paper used in this book meets the minimum requirements of ANSI/NISO Z39.48-1992 (R1997) (Permanence of Paper).

Library of Congress Cataloging-in-Publication Data

Names: Stratis, Niko, author.
Title: The dad rock that made me a woman / Niko Stratis.
Other titles: American music series (Austin, Tex.)
Description: First edition. | Austin : University of Texas Press, 2025. | Series: American music series
Identifiers: LCCN 2024036136 (print) | LCCN 2024036137 (ebook)
ISBN 978-1-4773-3148-4 (hardcover)
ISBN 978-1-4773-3149-1 (pdf)
ISBN 978-1-4773-3150-7 (epub)
Subjects: LCSH: Stratis, Niko. | Rock music fans—Biography. | Transgender women—Biography. | Rock music—History and criticism.
Classification: LCC ML429.S8915 A3 2025 (print) | LCC ML429.S8915 (ebook) | DDC 782.42166092—dcundefined
LC record available at https://lccn.loc.gov/2024036136
LC ebook record available at https://lccn.loc.gov/2024036137

doi:10.7560/331484

To my mom and dad.

Thank you for being patient with
me while I figured it out.

I always assumed that that's how it was in every family. But when I see the warmth, closeness, the fun of your relationship. . . . My father's a good man. He always wanted what was best for me. But where I have a father, you have a dad.

—MAJOR CHARLES EMERSON WINCHESTER III,
*M*A*S*H*, "Sons and Bowlers,"
episode 20, season 10

Contents

Far away from dry land, and its bitter memories 1

Bitter melodies, turning your orbit around 9

The whole world will be listening now 27

Got to be something better than in the middle 41

Why the hell are you so sad? 55

If I could be who you wanted, all the time 73

See you in heaven if you make the list 91

He might be a father but he sure ain't a dad 103

Last night I dreamt I'd forgotten my name 118

Take my hand and help me not to shake 130

Play with matches if you think you need to play with matches 141

I can't think of floorboards anymore 158

I'm ready for both of us now 168

Want to change my clothes, my hair, my face 177

Pick up the pieces and go home 191

It's the mercy I can't take 201

We're all supposed to try 216

I wanna see it when you find out what comets, stars, and moons are all about 224

I never thought about love when I thought about home 232

If the dead just go on living, well there's nothing left to fear 245

The Dad Rock That Made Me a Woman

Far away from dry land, and its bitter memories

"FISHERMAN'S BLUES"
THE WATERBOYS

There's a mythical mixtape that we lost. Lost from its home in the dashboard of my dad's old work truck: a white and rust 1988 Chevy S-10 with a bench seat, no power steering, an AM radio, and a cassette deck. A tape so expertly crafted by my father that all the guys who worked in the glass shop—the one he managed for decades on Fourth Avenue, right down the street from the good bakery and the pet store that's never open—would pretend they had work to do just so they could drive around downtown Whitehorse and listen to it.

On the long summer days, when the sun lodged itself high in the sky and never came down, you could see an All West Glass truck with the window down blaring "Guess That's Why

They Call It the Blues" by Elton John from a manual winding window. My dad never liked to have the extravagance of modern convenience in the bones of a work truck, and it was by a stroke of luck that this truck had a tape deck at all.

When I think about dad rock, I think about the music of my father.

Dad rock is a genre of loose origin and even looser definition, a box with blurred lines and fuzzy edges letting all things bleed in and out of it at will. The classic definition of the genre is born in garages, the golden age of AM radio, and air stained by the smell of cheap beer lingering in bronze bottles. Records you could buy for a dollar in any record store with your eyes closed, soaring guitar solos and anthemic classics that play well at any wedding around 9:30 p.m., before everyone is so drunk that they would like to make some regrettable memories but deep enough into the night that somebody is showing how little they have learned about dancing.

My dad never listened to this kind of music, never spent time in a garage clad in hobbies and memories with an old radio and a car he swears will run one day. He quit drinking before I was born, never partied much. My dad has always been quiet, chatty but only if you push him to talk. He enjoys a cup of good coffee more than any other drink you could offer.

My parents still live in the house I grew up in, on a quiet street in a residential area of Whitehorse, Yukon, Canada. The backyard was rock and stone when we moved in, and slowly over years the soil was tilled and toiled and covered in sod to transform it into something more. A garage sits there, too, at the end of a gravel driveway, but there has never been a car inside of it and the only radio in it has never really worked.

My father never felt much need to spend a lot of time in there either.

Instead, he spent what few hours he wasn't at work safely inside, with the stereo in the corner of a living room that has, in the years between then and now, been renovated time and again to remove all shades and tints of the memories that it held. The golden shag carpet and the brown tiles on the floor, all the light tinted in amber and technicolor. All of it gone, but still there if I stand far enough away and remember it how it was.

So much of my relationship to music is driven by what it says about who I am. What the things I collect and adore can possibly say about the parts of myself I am desperate for people to see. My dad has always taken to music privately. His albums weren't on display and his music was played more often in headphones than in speakers, loud enough for him and no one else.

My father is, in fact, a largely private man. He is no doubt reading this right now and not entirely comfortable that I am writing about him at all. Hi, Dad. I am writing about you here because this is a book about dad rock and you are my dad and this was an unavoidable crossroads. I apologize.

When we were kids we had a stereo that sat in the corner of the living room, a dusty silver Sanyo stack that had an amp, a double-deck cassette rack, a CD player, and a turntable. The stereo stand my dad made himself, out of window and door molding from the glass shop that he stained a dark brown and bronze glass shelves. My father is a man who loves to make something for himself above all else, trusting few to be able to create what he knows himself to be perfectly capable of.

I know what music he listened to partly because the detritus of his habits were always there. CDs by the Waterboys and

Gordon Lightfoot remained behind when he spent long days and quiet evenings away at work. I know “Fisherman’s Blues” as the song that escaped his headphones late at night when he wasn’t working and was trying his best to relax; he would lie in the corner on a big green pillow with a book open and face down on his chest and headphones protecting his ears while he napped.

My mom tells me that my dad got into record collecting not through fierce loyalty to an artist, but because he was driven by a chaos engine of whimsy and desire. All it took was an album cover that caught his eye, a band name or an album title that was just clever enough to never be forgotten, and he would buy it. The Ozark Mountain Daredevils, or Dan Hicks and His Hot Licks.

My dad never drank and never really threw parties, but my parents did on occasion have people over to sit and talk, and for these events he made mixtapes. Elaborate mixtapes that had Sade and Tears for Fears and Elton John songs that weren’t the big hits. When a lot of people talk about dad rock, they are talking about the kind of homogenous version of rock and roll that all sounds a little like bands trying to be Wings after Paul McCartney was through with the idea, but the dad rock in my house was often songs like “Sweetest Taboo.”

I don’t always have a great memory; sometimes it takes great skill and concentration to remember anything that happened to me in the years before this one. Music always brings me back to this place. I forgot a lot of my past, but that’s not to say that it is gone. It lives in fits and starts whenever conjured by the right song hitting me at the right time.

I was on a drive, years ago now, on a highway in the Yukon in the dead of winter. There was a door in need of repair in a post office in the small town of Mayo, six hours north of

Whitehorse. If you're driving on the highway toward Dawson City, you'll eventually hit a crossroads after a bridge. Go left, you'll head to Dawson. Turn right, and you'll head to Mayo. Population around 490.

Pretty good pizza, if you get there at the right time of year.

I was on the highway by myself, driving my midnight blue 2012 Toyota Tundra along the endless repeating scenery in dulled silence. The Yukon is famous for its beauty, and the rumors are in fact true. It's just that so many remarkable and beautiful things are often boring with repeated viewings. Bring a lot of coffee for the drive and trust me that it helps.

It was just me, my coffee, and my click wheel iPod connected by a flimsy cable to the onboard stereo. Bluetooth connectivity and streaming services don't mean much on long highways with no Wi-Fi. My dad always had a tape, and I've always got an iPod. My dad likes to remind me to always be prepared, and I am always prepared to be alone.

There is something in a drive through frozen wilderness, where the temperature gauge on your dashboard tells you the air outside is sitting crisp and still at 36 degrees below zero. Where the heat blowing in through air vents has settled in nicely and you don't need a jacket. The air blue-black in low light. The winter never sees much of the sun. Just me and an iPod on shuffle conjuring memories and beloved favorites.

That drive, that day, I was thinking about the end of all things. I had begun to wonder what would happen if I told everyone the truth about myself. The fallout of a life lived as a lie. The loss of friends, the abandonment of families.

"Fisherman's Blues" by Irish-British band the Waterboys shifted into the stereo speakers, perfectly balanced between front and back, left and right. The Waterboys have seen different lives lived under the same name. At times a grandiose display of stadium rock, others more subdued and traditional, pensive and reflective. Their name means different things to different people. The list of former members on the band's Wikipedia page reads like the ledger of all the surviving residents in a town only big enough for them.

Memories of my dad bleed from "Fisherman's Blues." A song that escaped his headphones at night, or played loudly through the stereo in the rare moments he played his music loud enough that we all might hear. Music often seemed to be just for him, just something he needed. Nothing more. There are few photos of him in our family records, but listen to this song and there he is, on the couch with a book folded on his chest. Tussled black hair, three-day stubble. Just resting his eyes, he would say, lying only a little. Finding rare pockets of peace within which to sleep away the exhaustion of all things.

It's a song about a relationship dissolving. Mike Scott, the only consistent member of the Waterboys through all its permutations, wrote it as the sound of the band was shifting in the late 1980s, away from keyboards and electric guitars to mandolins and fiddles. Something different, something closer to home maybe. It's about a relationship falling apart, about the strength needed to find change and keep moving.

And I know I will be loosened,
From the bonds that hold me fast,
And the chains all around me,
Will fall away at last.

I thought about dying. About disappearing. What it means to be alive and be nothing to everyone you have ever known.

Remember when the house used to look different. The light, warm and amber. The carpet was different then. Wallpaper and a different table and the microwave that was so old and heavy that none of us trusted using it. Remember how Dad had to throw it away and how even he thought it was too heavy.

Remember the stereo in the corner, long gone now, remember Dad playing music on the weekend when he was home, lying on the couch reading a book about climbing Mount Everest or thinking about kayaking. Mom in the kitchen making scones, or maybe muffins. Maybe she was in the hospital. That started to happen a lot in those days. Remember a perfect and peaceful afternoon or late evening.

I have collected memories in songs for as long as I can remember, and on this drive down this lonely stretch of Yukon highway late in the winter I thought about the tape long lost from my dad's old truck. That truck is gone now, too, crushed into a cube after it died on the highway in Calgary in 2002. I thought about my dad, my mom, the memories of our lives as they shift and fade in my mind. I thought about what will happen when they learn the truth. And how these memories might be all I'm left with.

My dad made mixtapes and I have never asked him why. I can only assume the answer, just as I did back when they played through the stereo speakers of my memories. Maybe he was always leaving these songs for people to hear, to learn through them and to take lessons from the songs captured to tape. Maybe this was how he communicated; maybe this was him telling me that he knew that our relationship might change someday but that he had left me all of these memories and lessons to guide me.

"Fisherman's Blues" sounds and feels like many things, and among those scattered emotions is a man seeking the solace of difficult work. What peace might escape working so hard to build a life, away from dry land and bitter memories. My dad taught me many things without speaking them aloud, and some of these lessons have taken me a lifetime to decipher. How to work hard, how to seek peace in hardship, find the things you love and let them soothe you. Let them remain with you forever.

A tape mixed by an expert craftsman that leads you through a life.

Bitter melodies, turning your orbit around

"JESUS, ETC."
WILCO

I allowed my brain the fine luxury of lying to my heart, sitting in the window seat of a twin-jet airplane flying south and then east, across the northern corner of British Columbia before circling farther down, crossing the invisible divide of the pretend provincial lines into Alberta, touching down on the tarmac in Edmonton. The entire flight I sat in solemn silence, staring out the window at the clouds as they swayed with gentle rhythm, aimlessly spinning the click wheel on a 32 GB iPod between playlists made for specific ventures. A playlist for the shower, a playlist for a long drive, and a playlist for the hour after getting home from work, before beginning the slow and steady process of getting blackout drunk. Playlists that reminded me of a youth that felt so far away, even though I was firmly in my mid-twenties.

As the wheels touched down and people rose eagerly from seats, preparing to take up space in the aisle so they could shove and cajole each other down a narrow hallway, I lingered and circled my fingers on the iPod wheel until it was no longer appropriate to still be on the airplane. The time had come to stand up and move out and see what reality was waiting for me outside the long bridge connecting the real world housed in the Edmonton airport and the utopia I was forming in seat 34D in the exit row by the wing.

I rose, slung a backpack over my shoulder, thanked the stewards as I ducked to clear the little airplane door that never expects you to be taller than five foot eleven. Watched each step of my boots down the aisle of the bridge and ran my fingers along the cold steel handrail and looked at the advertisements urging young people to move to Alberta and work themselves to death for profit in the oil sands. I emerged into an airport lounge filled with people rushing to each other, hugging and crying and laughing. Everyone here to see someone else. Everyone aside from me, standing and crying to myself in the lobby of the Edmonton airport with no one to greet, no one to hug me and tell me how much they missed me. My body expected her to be here to do just that, all part of the great lie cooked up by a brain moving through all five stages, tentatively crossing the gate into acceptance.

Jane was really dead.

I spun my fingers around my iPod once more, found W in the artists section, and spun through to Wilco. I spun once more to *Yankee Hotel Foxtrot*, then around to "Jesus, etc.," and watched people holding their hands over their mouths the way people politely laugh at strangers crying in public, waited for my bag to join me in being the last off the plane and into the building. Wilco had become a band of great importance to me as I moved into my mid-twenties and felt myself becoming more of an adult. Someone with a life of responsibility and desire seeking music that reflected this changing status, craving a bridge between the recklessness of youth and the weight of growing older.

Wilco is proof that there is something good to come out of the kind of breakup that feels like it might end you forever. Front man and primary songwriter Jeff Tweedy had been a founding member of Uncle Tupelo, the alt-country band that was so influential a magazine was named after their debut record, *No Depression*. Tweedy and Uncle Tupelo's Jay Farrar developed a contentious relationship as the band found fame and Tweedy developed as a voice and songwriter to pay attention to. The two would shout at each other on tour, reprimand each other backstage, and trade barbs through the voice of their manager before they decided to split once and for all. Farrar went off to form his own band, Son Volt, and Tweedy, claiming the remains of his former band in the divorce, created Wilco, named for a military pro word that means "will comply."

I had told Jane that I would be back, and it was the last lie I ever told her. We had met in 2003, at a pool table in a high-end bar for fake cowboys in downtown Edmonton on a Thursday night. We bonded over a shared love of chicken wings, conspiracy theories around the death of Kurt Cobain, and a distrust of guys in $400 jeans riding a mechanical bull off to the side of a dance floor no one ever used. That night we shared phone numbers written on the last scraps of a coaster and called each other from cab rides heading in opposite directions to make plans to play mini golf in the West Edmonton Mall the following Saturday.

I bought the first line of camera phones from Motorola the morning of our first date, replacing the cell phone that fell out of my pocket while riding a swing stage up the side of a high-rise building I worked on at the time. This is how I know that companies can brag all they like that their phones, the yellow and black ones that are rugged and designed for the daily rigors of the Working Man, can survive most things, but they cannot survive a 374-foot fall onto the dirt below. Trust me, that phone, like all things that fall from the grace of great heights, is gone for good.

My first camera phone had a 4 megapixel lens on the outside and no easy way to take photos off of it, but the novelty was an obsession and the first photo on the first camera phone I ever had was Jane on our first date giving me the finger on hole 3 of the mini golf course inside the West Edmonton Mall, right by the pirate ship and where the dolphins are on occasion. No one tells you where the dolphins go when they disappear. Some days, everything beautiful is just gone and you might never know why. Like a cell phone or a dolphin or a relationship you were certain would last forever.

Farrar and Tweedy split and formed their own bands, and while Son Volt found itself with some fame, it was Wilco that really took off as the commercial success. I have to imagine that this never sat well with Farrar, who was already jealous of the rising star in Tweedy's limitless talent. The first Wilco record, *A.M.*, released in 1995, was received fairly well but not so well that it changed the landscape they were looking to form. It's hard to do anything after the breakup of a pairing that a lot of external forces had invested stakes in. People praised the sound, which was grown in the country and roots soil of Gram Parsons and Neil Young, and it was fine and good but never fully transcendent.

In 1997, Tweedy began working with the multi-instrumentalist Jay Bennet, and with the release of *Being There* Wilco began to find themselves leaning in new sonic directions, incorporating power pop and psych and punk rock as well as the alt-country they were born of. It became impossible to ignore that Wilco was here to shift tectonic plates, form a new landmass for eager hearts to dwell and thrive on. On *Being There*, Tweedy was now thirty years old, a young parent managing the anxieties of an uncertain start to a new band and the responsibilities of being an adult with a house and bills. A new dad placing all of his eggs in the basket of playing in a successful rock and roll band.

My dad worked in a glass shop most of his life. When he was around thirteen, he and his brother stepped in to help run the family shop they lived above, in an old, converted firehouse in downtown Vancouver that his family moved into after they emigrated from Cardiff after World War II. My grandfather turned the space into a glass shop. My dad learned the trade within the walls of this shop alongside his brother before he met my mother and fell in love and moved from small town to small town throughout the British Columbian interior. They had a shotgun wedding followed shortly by the birth of my sister in Williams Lake and then me, born in Terrace, British Columbia, in June 1982.

In 1988, in the dead of a cold and bitter winter, we moved to a small brown house with turquoise trim and a front door in the back of the house on a residential street in the Yukon, across the street from the Yukon River. The backyard had no grass, all rocks and loose soil and sharp objects, but we didn't know that yet. The ground lay still with its secrets, hard and frozen and foreboding.

I was only partly through kindergarten when we moved, and that winter I started at a new school that was just up the street from our house, in a series of decommissioned ATCO trailers positioned on top of wooden blocks. Each trailer held a single grade, save one that was for both the first and second grade and the site of my only academic achievement, where I accidentally did the entire second grade when I was supposed to do the first. I was told I was predominantly accelerated, a gifted child capable of gifted things, and they offered to put me ahead, to the third or even the fourth grade. My mom said no, she was already concerned with my limited ability to socialize and with the growing severity of my anxieties, and she worried that pushing me ahead would only stunt my emotional growth. I didn't talk much to anyone, and every lunch and recess I walked out by myself to a fence on the outskirts of the playground and kicked a fence board by myself until it was time to go back inside and feel forgotten.

Wilco's third album, 1999's *Summerteeth*, was the first time the band proved they were capable of lush and dangerous beauty. Tweedy wanted to improve as a writer and focused on the great works of literature to color in the boundaries of his voice, and what emerged is a sprawling and grand portrait of technicolor songwriting that proved that Wilco was always capable of writing a hit and had simply been choosing not to. Where Wilco had always been a band that emerged from the belly of alt-country creation, now we were seeing and hearing not just what the genre was capable of but what was lying in their influences. Where Gram Parsons and Neil Young were boxes long checked on a list of influences, shades of Jeff Lynne, the most eclectic madness of Brian Wilson and the wildest impulses of Big Star started to emerge. Shades of the golden age of rock music that thrived as it blew through the high end of cheap speakers in garages held sacred by the dads I imagined everyone else but me grew up with.

Summerteeth touched on the insecurities of a young dad in a rock and roll band. Jeff Tweedy was starting to become unraveled from time on the road, anxious and depressed from time away from his family. Wilco was aging and struggling with the effects of time on their hearts and souls, and this spills out and fills in all the cracks of their foundation to build something sturdy and concrete on. The term wouldn't be given to them until much later, but Wilco became a dad rock band the minute they became fathers and the second they dedicated themselves to the necessary perils of being dads.

My dad wasn't at home as much as he would have liked when I was growing up. As we entered the 1990s, we hit first a recession and then my mother's faltering health. In my early teen years, she was diagnosed with Crohn's disease. I didn't know what it was, just that it meant she was in the hospital a lot, and my dad worked extra hard to cover the downsizing of our household income. Like my dad before me, I got my first job when I was thirteen. Not in the glass shop, at least not at first. First it was a grocery store, then fashion retail, and then in 1999 the glass shop. I became an apprentice in a trade I took up because I didn't know who I was and finding shades of my father to emulate felt like the best option to fall into.

The first time I ever left home for somewhere else, the Twin Towers fell in New York City. I woke up on September 11, 2001, with no knowledge of what was happening, just a pressing need to leave home. My mom was in the hospital, my dad was at work, and with neither of them home the house sat lifeless. Even the worst news never finds us in silence. I left the house with visions of escape in my heart and my 1988 Datsun Maxima ready for the road ahead, its metallic baby blue exterior announcing my personality in a cavalcade of stickers purchased from Interpunk.com, the internet's foremost punk rock superstore.

That morning I drove away from our family home in Riverdale, the residential area of Whitehorse nestled away by the Yukon River, down a street I walked every day on my way to school despite never knowing its name. I think it's Nisutlin, but don't quote me on that. I got down to the Super A, took a left, down another street with an unknowable name that traveled past F. H. Collins, the high school I failed to graduate on time from. Drove past the skate park where that kid got blown up by a pipe bomb one time during an interschool rumble, across the street from the road leading up to the hospital.

Across the Yukon River bridge and downtown to where goodbyes begin.

The first house I arrived at, I knocked and could hear frantic noises emerging from somewhere inside, then a door flung open and my friend's French-Canadian mother who forgot we had a language barrier spoke in rushed français and pointed at a TV where the second plane hit the towers. It didn't matter that neither of us understood each other; none of us knew what to say anyway. We watched, stunned and shaken, and then made awkward farewells in the living room, the air stained by the smell of toast that burned while we clung to the TV.

I stopped to see my dad at the glass shop next. He was working with the big green garage doors flung open wide and the radio playing louder than normal. He shook my hand, wished me good luck and safe travels, and laughed and told me this was the best day at work he ever had. No one to bother him. It was the first time I had ever seen him listen to music in the shop without me, and it was the first time he looked like the kind of dad I imagined everyone else had. We said our farewells, and then I was gone.

In September 2001, Wilco released *Yankee Hotel Foxtrot* for free on their website after a contentious split with Reprise, their now former record label. It was supposed to drop on the eleventh but got delayed and turned around with a change in labels, and the advent of the internet and file sharing meant that fans were downloading low-quality MP3s that appeared on copycats of the recently disgraced peer-to-peer service Napster. Not wanting their fans to be listening to the album with less quality than it deserved, the band put the whole thing on their website, letting fans simply surf to WilcoWorld .net to listen to it for free.

Yankee Hotel Foxtrot is Wilco's Dorian Gray, ageless and beautiful and full of secrets and wonder. Long held as the masterpiece of the band's many creations, it was recorded in the midst of new upheaval in the band as Tweedy split with longtime collaborator Jay Bennet and also from Reprise Records in a battle about what Wilco was and what they might yet become. An album questioning and challenging who we will grow to be as we cling to all we've known with desperation.

My dad never asked me to follow in his footsteps; I just always assumed I was supposed to. I was supposed to be a son, supposed to become a man. Men and sons follow their fathers. Trust the process, never question its logic. My dad had always done this work, and so I should too.

Yankee Hotel Foxtrot opens sparse, percussive, and somber. Like driving through a low-hanging fog in the rain in the early morning. "I Am Trying to Break Your Heart" is the lead track, the opening statement. Here, Wilco works to break you down to nothing.

Jane and I had shared a love of musical conspiracy theories, and there were little whispers around this record and 9/11. How closely tied it all felt. The iconic cover with a photo of the twin towers of the Marina City complex in Chicago. A song called "Ashes of American Flags." The line from the album's stunning centerpiece, "Jesus, etc."

Tall buildings shake,
Voices escape, singing sad sad songs.

Yankee Hotel Foxtrot is Wilco building a new home on a beach formed by shifting sands. Frantic and reserved, anxious and chaotic, and calm and beautiful all at once. A whole and complete sound built in a time of uncertain difficulty. Seizing opportunity in a tailspin.

I only ever felt comfortable with change if it already felt familiar. I left home, moved to Alberta. Attended trade school and learned the tools of my father and his before him. People remarked that there are so few third-generation glaziers. It is difficult and precarious work, the kind we often urge people to avoid. Find a life different than this one of great danger. But I never questioned it, never asked my dad what he thought. What he thought of this work, of me, of this life. I just accepted it. Never changed. Fell into a life.

There is a history of alcoholism and addiction in this trade. This is true of a lot of trades, but glass is what I saw everything through. In 2003 I worked with a man with a scar along the back of his neck. He had stuck his head through an opening in a broken window to survey the frame on the other side and in doing so dislodged the glass above and it came down on him like an ineffective guillotine. He drank a lot to avoid processing how these brushes with death might leave their marks on us. I joined him.

There's a history of substance use in Wilco's trade too. *Yankee Hotel Foxtrot* opened the conversation on the troubles it might bring. An energy you can see clearly in the rearview, sparks outlining anxieties and depressions that feel heightened by parties that may have lasted a little too long. A buzz, a hum. Tweedy's songwriting is more eloquent here, bold and poetic. Angry at times, pensive in others.

All my lies are always wishes
I know I would die if I could come back new.

There's a desperation there, too, that feeling of holding onto the steering wheel of a car skidding on an icy road. The urge to hold on, knowing that one way or another, you'll need to let go.

In an autobiography written years later, Tweedy wonders if his migraines, which led to his addictions, stemmed from mood disorders shared down a family line. I wonder this too. I had this same hum all my life. It gets louder—all hums do when you don't locate their source.

My dad quit drinking before I was born, and from what I know of his father, he drank until he was gone from this earth. There is something in our blood, I worry. I am a third-generation glazier; am I a third-generation problem drinker? Soothing anxieties and depressions with alcohol and drugs. Just enough to feel nothing. Just enough to appear alive and dead all at once.

In 2004, Jeff Tweedy went into rehab for an addiction to painkillers, the same year Wilco released their highly anticipated follow-up to *Yankee Hotel Foxtrot*: *A Ghost Is Born*. Where there was a hum in the backdrop of *Yankee Hotel Foxtrot*, now there was a persistent buzz. It's a frantic record that illuminates the pain caged in Tweedy at the time. In the rearview, he has talked about not wanting to make the record while high, and the buzz and bombast of its loudest pieces are cacophonous rhythms born of incessant headaches and anxiety. The soundtrack to a man pinned down by the weight of what often felt like the end. Tweedy thought he was going to die, made a record of his loudest and more dire thoughts as a legacy for his children to find and build a memory of their father from.

Death lingers in this era of Wilco. Death lingers in our lives, and still we wonder at its arrival. What will they make of the secrets we leave in all the bones of our bodies left behind?

In 2004 Jane and I split up. I felt I had to follow my dad into the world he had built for himself, and that meant leaving Edmonton behind, moving back to the Yukon. Walking back onto the streets whose names I never learned that will always remember my feet.

That year marks the first time I can remember not recalling where I had been all night. I woke up in a bed in a friend's basement, walked into the downstairs bathroom. Looked at my face in the mirror, sunken eyes, scrappy beard. I said "fuck" as I read it written on my knuckles in permanent marker, only partially covered in blood.

The night before we had been at a party. There was a hum. I was feeling anxious, lonely, sad. There was a hum. I drank, tequila, beer, shots. Did drugs in the bathroom. There was a hum. Tequila. Rum. Beer. There was a hum. Someone found a longboard. We found two. Went out into the street with them. There was a hum. We skated for a bit, but my friend Sarah decided it was sketchy to longboard with a hum vibrating our bodies. She went inside. I opted to stay out there. I'm told I walked into the house a half hour later clutching my arm to hold in the blood, asking if anyone had any paper towels. I had skated into a parked motorcycle; my body flew over the bike and hit the curb on the other side. Someone helped me bandage my arm. I think. The faces start to blur. There was a hum. I drank. Tequila. Beer. I think.

There was a hum.

There's a photo preserved somewhere of my body on a couch under a pile of things. Coats. Pillows. A coffee table. A TV left turned on. The DVD logo bouncing around, waiting to hit the corner of the screen. The hum blurs out the memory of this event that I lived through. Erased with booze and bathroom drugs. For a long time after, Sarah called me Fuck Knuckles. I thought about getting that tattooed. Take this haunting memory of immense shame and brand myself with it. Steer into the skid.

Drinking drowns out the hum, dulls the persistent buzz. Listening to *A Ghost Is Born*, the hum and buzz are all too clear, Tweedy wrestling with the pain and anxiety lingering within. The ghost is born, the ghost is here. A hum. A buzz. Even in its quiet moments, like on "Handshake Drugs" and "Muzzle of Bees," the noise finds a way in. The hum and the buzz appear. They haunt this place; they are a part of the story. They leave marks on a map to show you where they have been. Tweedy wanted to leave these songs to his sons when he died young, as he thought he would, so they could piece him together and build something of his life in his absence. A dad teaching through pain and hardship, lessons learned through life's hardest methods.

That same year, 2004, he checked himself into a dual rehab clinic. He was eager to make sure the ghost was not yet him.

I hadn't yet learned the lessons I needed to survive. I drank more. Partied more. Took more responsibility at the glass shop to take over for my father and continue the family tradition of glass work and drinking until it's time to stop. I got so drunk on a Friday night that my coworker found me asleep on the glass cutting table in the shop on Saturday morning. I didn't want to walk home, so I just brushed most of the glass away and slept on its carpeted surface.

One weekend I woke up in a stranger's basement, walked upstairs to see them making a nice breakfast for themselves. They weren't surprised or shocked to see me. Made me coffee. Asked if I was okay. I had thought their home was mine. They could see I was in crisis and let me sleep on their couch.

Fuck Knuckles strikes again.

The kindness of strangers keeping me alive.

Jane and I reconnected in 2006 when I had to go back to Edmonton for work for a few months. I hesitantly emailed her old Hotmail address. To my eternal surprise she responded. We made plans. Dinner at a Mexican restaurant out by a bowling alley. When I picked her up, I commented on her new black hair color, a stark contrast to the blonde she had been when we were together. She awkwardly brushed it off. We drove to the restaurant, chatted and laughed and filled each other in on the gaps in the time since we last saw the other. She had a boyfriend, but they had split up. I had a few partners that never worked out as well.

Everything I had missed about her came rushing back, and I built a future for us in my head as we drove to dinner.

We sat in the Mexican restaurant and watched plates of fajitas move by as she mustered the courage to break the air, and she told me she had cancer right as the waiter came to ask if we were ready. We were not.

The black hair was a wig. It's hard to get real hair blonde wigs, so she had decided to just go for dark hair instead. The future I had so recently laid out for us shifted in my mind. I was barely old enough to grapple with the reality of this situation. She had cancer. It was in remission, but she wasn't out of the woods yet. She still had to go to the cancer center in Edmonton to get treatment on a regular basis. But she was fine, really.

We hung out a lot, as friends. Went on dates, as friends. We went to the movies a lot. Jane liked to joke about her cancer; maybe it helped her disarm the gravity of it all. We were in line to get popcorn to give us the strength needed to get through *Clerks 2*, the line moving not quick enough for us to make our movie on time, and I joked that she was going to die of cancer before we got served. A woman in front of us turned and started screaming at us about how insensitive I was to real cancer patients. Jane took her wig off and said, "It's fine, I'm actually dying, so don't worry about it."

I could never tell her how I felt. I went to visit her at the cancer center. She had friends come down in a hurry to do her makeup before I got there. I didn't know this until later, after the funeral. I lied; I told her I was in love with someone back home. I left Edmonton again. Promised to come back. We hugged. I kissed her just once.

We kept in touch. Long calls on weekends that became harder to schedule. I wouldn't hear from her for a week, would check obituaries for her name and then go out and drink to drown out the hum. Once I got her on the phone and her voice was shaky, rough, and sullen. She was on a lot of painkillers, she told me. Her arm was being amputated in the morning in a desperate bid to save her life. The cancer had come back. It was spreading. I wished her good luck. I'll be thinking of you, I said. She asked me to call her the next week. Maybe we could make plans and I could come down and visit. Check in, okay?

I learned that Jane had died in the early hours of the morning one day in May 2007. My phone buzzing in my pocket woke me up, face down on the lawn in front of the house I lived in the basement of. I must have passed out, rolled out of a cab. Drank the hum away. Jane's dad called to tell me she had passed away peacefully, surrounded by family. She had asked him to call me to say goodbye.

I never got to say it back.

In 2007, Wilco released *Sky Blue Sky*. From the outset, a more subdued effort from the anxious noise of their previous two outings. Album opener "Either Way" blooms softly:

Maybe the sun will shine today.

In the intervening years since *A Ghost Is Born*, Wilco had grown into themselves as a band. Tweedy had gone through rehab and emerged as a more focused and eager songwriter. He had written *A Ghost Is Born* as a farewell, and now he was here to find what voice he is capable of wielding as time moves forward. As he ages, as his sons age alongside him. As he is able to show them the way, the path he walked, the roads he took. Where he stumbled and fell.

In a review for *Pitchfork*, Rob Mitchum called it "an album of unapologetic straightforwardness." He wrote, "*Sky Blue Sky* nakedly exposes the dad-rock gene Wilco has always carried but courageously attempted to disguise."

Wilco becomes dad rock, and *dad rock* becomes a pejorative. *Dad* becomes something scathing, a term with teeth and bitter scars. How dare they become something so lifeless and straightforward.

They had never been trying to hide their dad rock gene, whatever that truly means. Many of them had been fathers long before 2007, but it's only once they had seemingly softened that being a dad became a mark against them. This was a band breathing freely after holding in air for so long, anxiously waiting for an implosion. Now they could relax. They could be soft. They could worry and fret at the state of the world and the exhaustion of all things without being haunted by the specter of death lurking around the corners ahead.

On "Sky Blue Sky," the album's title track, Tweedy looks back at his home of Belleville, Illinois. Recalling an old parade, the gray sky. The battered windows, the streets that felt sad and empty. How it was time to move on, find somewhere new, learn how to build a life on new streets. A survivor seeking joy even in all the gray and darkness.

I survived, it's good enough for now.

There is a realism in Tweedy's work here, perhaps tempered by his recent rehab and battle with addiction. This idea of believing you're going to die and then not suffering that loss. How to move on with time you never imagined possible. This is a dad showing the way. Look at the work left behind; look at all the places I fell and stumbled. Look where the anxiety nearly claimed me. Hear the hum and buzz wail in these notes. And know that I made it here.

With a sky blue sky, this rotten time.

There's a delightful cynic in Tweedy's work, always with a little hope blended in to thicken the water. Seeking something to live for, unafraid to remember all the difficult places that built to this point. This is a dad, showing a life, showing how to fight for satisfaction.

My dad never tried to warn me away from the pitfalls of this world. Never tried to push me into anything or made demands of my time. I think he maybe struggled with the limits of what he could teach me, and instead he chose to lead by example. He shows great love with tender actions when I am unaware I need support to hold the walls of my heart in place. He has lived a life that has seen hard and difficult corners but arrived with a spirit tempered by survival. Learned by failing, lessons gained in the collapse. Dad rock exemplifies this ideal, an earnest spirit made quiet and calm, finally able to breathe out and share words of gentle encouragement on how to keep going. It's good enough for now.

The whole world will be listening now

"BRAIN OF J"
PEARL JAM

McDonald's was my first and most jarring rejection, or at least that's what my memory allows me to recall. I'm sure I had been rejected before that moment for a great many reasons, but it's the rejection from the McDonald's of my youth that I remember.

I was thirteen years old and needed a job, which I thought was a perfectly normal thing for a thirteen-year-old kid to need and to attain and only in hindsight is a sign that we didn't always have a lot of money in the house when I was a kid. I wanted to have spare money for food and CDs and clothes, and the only way I was going to be able to keep my habits afloat was by working. I applied for a job at McDonald's without any preparation or forethought. I assumed the process would be like ordering food; walk in, announce your desires to someone behind the counter, and they will bring it to you in short order. I asked for an application, filled out my name and address and home phone number, lied on the line for Social Insurance Number because I did not have one—my fake one had a D in it, which no SIN in Canada (a series of nine numbers and absolutely no letters) would ever have—and slid it across the counter with an unearned confidence in my prospects as a new hire.

"You're just not what we're looking for" is the kindest way you can say, "You have got to be fucking kidding me" to a child.

I'm not entirely sure this is how the story goes anymore; it was 1995 then and it is not 1995 now, and with time these stories shift and change, become fading photographs of themselves. No less foundational, no less real, but washed-out colors and shapes that recall a life. Tender memories of hardships, setbacks, and triumphs to mark on the wall and show how we've grown. I will never remember everything perfectly as it was, and it no longer matters how perfect the memory; it's the impact that's important.

I didn't like Eddie Vedder when he arrived on the scene because I felt that I was supposed to dislike him. Pearl Jam surfaced with *Ten* in 1991 in the rising tide of Nirvana's landmark *Nevermind*, and if you were just obsessed enough with one or the other you had to draw a line in the sand for yourself, decide on which side of it you would stand to fight a war no one conscripted you into.

I was young and eagerly impressionable at just the right time to be influenced by Nirvana and Cobain, took careful note of all the things he said he liked and didn't. R.E.M. and the Pixies, how to effortlessly hold cigarettes in your fingers. These became easy fascinations. With Pearl Jam, and the early

'90s major label push to replicate a sound emerging from the Pacific Northwest they could capitalize on, I learned how to pretend to be critical. Cobain didn't like bands like Pearl Jam and Alice in Chains, and so I didn't like bands like Pearl Jam and Alice in Chains. My opinions were just carbon copies of someone else's, watching them move and act and speak and aping their cues.

My earliest lessons were always from men. Men I was eager to emulate in order to find some secret path to understanding myself as a collection of men's parts and pieces gathered into a body that felt all together unbound. Like Frankenstein before the sewing and the electricity of it all. I rarely had the language to describe why I felt out of sync with myself, my gender, my sexuality, but the knowledge that I always felt wrong stuck to my ribs. A man rejected me from a job at McDonald's, but another saw potential hiding in all my unsewn parts and hired me for my first job: stock boy at Food Fair, the locally owned grocery store on Second Avenue downtown, where my mom went when she needed to do a big shop.

The owners at Food Fair stalked the store during the day, always said hi to my mom when we were there. It felt like walking in the shade of celebrity when it happened, like you were in the presence of royalty while holding on to a cold metal cart with a wobbling wheel. It wasn't until later that I learned how they said hi to anyone they didn't know to make them feel remembered, to encourage them to shop there more often. All Cheshire Cat smiles hiding rows of sharpened teeth, kind and warm and hungry, and they were more than happy to have another minimum wage worker on the floor if it kept one more mom coming through the door with money to spend.

Before chain stores moved into the city, Whitehorse was a collection of locally owned shops small and big, each catering to an individual's wants, needs, and distance. If you needed just a few items, you got your groceries at a smaller shop closer to home. The IGA or Riverdale Market next to the short-lived all-ages dance club owned by the guy who owned the bowling alley and the video store. If your needs were great, you went downtown to the Food Fair, or the Extra Foods next to the Coffee, Tea & Spice that always smelled exactly like the name would have you believe.

Downtown Whitehorse has changed a lot in the years since I was young, but I remember the way these rooms and buildings smelled. Their memories have stayed alive in my senses like an obstinate flame. The smell of the ground coffee and pungent teas blending with dirt and Mr. Clean on the cold tile floor in the mall, the crunch of snow under your boots in the dead of winter packed hard by car tires, the noxious smell of exhaust filtering the crisp air on Main Street in front of the bookstore, where trucks idled in the cold.

I used to steal copies of *Spin* and *Rolling Stone* from the Macs Fireweed on Main Street because they were too expensive, and because money was scarce but I craved the stories in their glossy pages. Long before the internet opened our lives to the possibility of eternal connectivity, we were left to gather facts for ourselves like wood for a long cold winter, and I stored the words and work of artists I adored like they might be the only flame that would keep me alive. Read about the rise of grunge, the death of hair metal, the glossy cover stories, the profiles on how a nobody from nowhere could become a cover star.

I wanted to dislike Eddie Vedder because Cobain didn't like Eddie Vedder, but I couldn't help but be intrigued by something in him, the secrets of a life unfolding on a page that gave new perspectives on every preconceived notion. Did you know that Eddie Vedder isn't even from fucking Seattle? Did you know that he grew up thinking a different man was his father, and that he didn't find out until his mother and stepfather divorced, but by the time he learned of his real father's existence the man had already died of multiple sclerosis? I wanted to hate Eddie Vedder, but his life became Shakespearean on the page.

While you were sittin' home alone at age thirteen,
Your real daddy was dyin'.

Vedder's real-life drama fueled the cathartic anger he sang with on inescapable hit singles like "Alive," his voice guttural one moment and soaring the next, like an angel falling to the earth.

You're still alive, she said, oh, and do I deserve to be?

I was hired on the spot at Food Fair in the late spring of 1995, despite still not having a Social Insurance Number, because bosses will always need laborers and they will always pay as little as legally possible for it. Minimum wage was $6.86 an hour, and I earned every cent of that stocking shelves after school: 3:15 until 6:00 p.m. Monday through Wednesday, 9:00 p.m. on Thursdays and Fridays.

I wasn't much of a talker for a very long time. When I was young my parents worried I might never speak, and it took me longer than normal to find my voice. My sister would often just announce my needs for me instead. I kept to myself, kept my head down, kept my thoughts inside. We didn't liberally use phrases like "undiagnosed anxiety disorder" in the mid-'90s, but it certainly would have helped to have some language to understand myself better. Working every day after school taught me many things, but the most important lesson was how to learn human interaction through endless repetition. Lessons are often best learned through failure, through understanding why you have fallen, and through learning to remember the heat of shame as it stings your skin so you might not repeat it again.

It took me a while to get into Pearl Jam. I liked *Ten* and *Vs.* just fine, but they didn't become mine the way music belongs to you when you're young and you need something to define the lines of your life. I liked Vedder's rage, how he was able to let fly a cathartic howl, like the demons he kept at bay were not content to just graze at the gates and left instead to roam. There's something otherworldly in his growling voice; words become muddled and unclear as he lets them free, as if he no longer has the energy to control his own pronunciations. There's something comically masculine about the early years of Pearl Jam, as if Vedder and crew—Stone Gossard, Jeff Ament, Mike McCready, and a revolving door of drummers starting with Jack Irons that ended with the lasting addition of former Soundgarden drummer Matt Cameron in 1998—were in on the joke of grunge overtaking the excessive masculinity of the '80s hair metal.

All my mentors at the grocery store were men, because this was the way of things. Men led men young and old into all the rooms and hallways they were meant to wander. A man led me through the swinging doors separating store from stockroom for the first time, showed me the receiving bay and the hallway where fresh stock was stored, the stairs leading up to the bathrooms that were also changing rooms to shift from civilian clothing to work-appropriate attire.

My first day on the job, I was late. The bus had decided not to run that day, which meant that my feet would have to instead, and I burst through the swinging doors into the back five minutes later than I wanted to be. My new boss, a hockey dad and hockey coach who rarely bothered to hide his sinister anger, was too busy to notice me arrive late. Too busy holding a man against the wall of the meat cooler. Too busy landing punches on the man's body to notice I was late. Too busy telling him that if he caught him stealing again he would kill him and no one would care. He showed me what he thought a man should be, this terrifying creation of fists and anger.

Pearl Jam and Nirvana were pitted against each other in the press as rising stars of a rapidly emerging movement. Nirvana positioned themselves as purists of the form, lambasting Pearl Jam as this corporate concoction of musicians designed only to sell records by copying a style that had only just started to become popular. By 1992 Cobain tried to soften those blows, saying that he had come to know Eddie Vedder and that he no longer felt inclined to attack him. That he felt bad for having been so aggressive toward this man he didn't know. This was a rare glimpse at a man admitting he was wrong in his anger.

It was months before my boss, the man who held another up against the wall, beating him in the stomach, found the same distaste for me that he did for everything he felt was weak. The grocery game is an easy one to master: stock shelves, turn all the products so the English side faces out, bag groceries, get carts, smile and say hello in that way that makes it seem like you remember everyone while learning no one's name. Hide your teeth behind your smile. I learned how I was perceived midday on a Saturday when new stock came into the store, when the specials for the week changed and the endcaps had to be redone.

Permit me a second to expand on my knowledge of the intricacies of the world of food retail. The endcap is the part at the end of the aisle that connects two aisles together, often stocked with a bunch of shit the store is desperate to get rid of to make room for anything else.

The endcaps had to be redone, and my boss tasked me with doing it all by myself for the first time to see just how capable I had become. I was older now, fourteen, with a few months working at the store under my belt. Growing tall, pretending to be strong, learning how to use my voice and move my body like all the other men so people would think I was one too. Maybe in lying to myself I could learn through everyone else how to sew together the parts of my body I didn't want or understand into something that made sense.

Eddie Vedder sounds angry in the first few Pearl Jam records. He was young and brash and immediately shouldered with terrible weights of fame, given a manufactured rivalry with another man equally young and brash and burdened. Montagues and Capulets. Catching him in snippets of live performances on stages around the world as *Ten* and then *Vs.* shot them to fame, he appeared a man possessed of furious anger. Never an anger aimed at someone, never anger as a weapon nor the anger of a strong hand, but the anger you come to understand if you learn the intricacies of violence hiding in the hearts of anxious and curious hearts. An anger at something burrowed into him that he could only process out loud.

The first time I designed an endcap all by myself, it looked terrible. I had never done it before, had only ever seen the result of someone else's work, and was tasked with reverse engineering success. I failed. My boss, a walking exaggeration of testosterone and strength, came over to inspect my work with his hand gently on my shoulders like a surveyor looking for flaws in a work in desperate process. A hand big and rough, with cracked and dry skin stretched tight over his palms. Skin like a desert longing for rain. His fingers slowly dug into my shoulders as he pointed out all my failings. His fingers moved up my shoulders to the back of my neck, tightened around it, and dug their tips into the soft crevices of my flesh as he pointed to where I had failed. They tightened further as he pointed to where I had been sloppy, where I had rushed. He could see that I rushed. His fingers tightened and it became hard to breathe. Couldn't I see how sloppy I had been? How bad I had been? How wrong I was? I couldn't really breathe. I was being paid good money to work here and this was the thanks they got for hiring me. A nothing kid with no experience or Social Insurance Number. I was so tall and skinny, so weak. I didn't even play hockey or act tough like the other men; I was bad at making an endcap and his fingers dug into my neck so hard I couldn't breathe, and I thought about him telling that man on my first day at work how no one would mourn his death. I thought about whether anyone would mourn mine.

A woman walked by and defused the situation. He said hi to her in that way that made her feel so special, like he had remembered her name, and he had no idea who the fuck she even was at all. She was as we all were, nothing in the strength of his hand. He released me. I gasped for air. I promised to be better.

Eddie Vedder sang ferocious, angry words searching for soft answers in hard places. On *Ten* he howled through the struggles with the very truth of his parentage ("Alive") and the terrible price of a young man's unchecked, violent anger and mental health struggles ("Jeremy"). Vedder looked outward, exploring imagined lives and possibilities beyond himself and his experiences. Beyond the way life moved to his rhythms. Like he was both teacher and student all at once, processing a relationship to the world the only way he knew how, giving breath to voices he could only try to comprehend.

I think there is anger in unknowing, anger in fear, anger in not having control. Anger in having control and it not being respected. My boss, the man who clasped his hand around my neck, craved control. When men gathered in the back room to sit on makeshift chairs and avoid work, they knew they only had to pretend to be talking about hockey to disarm his anger. He had almost gone pro, you know, but an injury sidelined him and now he was here. In a grocery store. Managing burn-out kids and young women and smiling at mothers whose names he would never remember. Beating up shoplifters in the back room and teaching young men how to be tough and strong by any means necessary. How to be just like him, just like he was supposed to be, when he played hockey, before he was denied some unseen greatness he felt he deserved.

Anger, like so many beautiful and dangerous things, is a spectrum. Anger comes from so many places, goes into so many dark corners. I understand anger because I have always felt it, always been drawn to it. Cobain was angry and I loved his fury. Anger at a world he could not control, that he could not always fit into, anger at himself. An anger turned inward. With Eddie Vedder I came to understand the catharsis that could come of anger. Of letting something out and knowing relief when it was all over.

I was angry after I got choked for not designing a perfect endcap but was unsure what to do with that emotion, the Newton's cradle it set into motion. A few months later, working with a man a few years older than me, a man adored by so many that I looked to him as the guiding light that might save me in this place, I let my enthusiasm get the better of me. I made too many jokes, maybe spoke too much, or too quickly. Maybe my voice was annoying. Maybe I was annoying. Factors combined into annoyance, and then suddenly he grabbed me and guided me into the stockroom, found a quiet corner, and worked out his frustrations with me in all the ways I would be sure to remember.

There is something in the way a man hits you when he wants the damage to be untold. He chooses careful targets. The stomach and the ribs and the places you can hide the damage. He was mindful to only wind me and to bruise me but to never mark me where it could be seen. I was told this was a lesson, that if I kept acting like I did someone would hurt me for real, that this wasn't for real, that he was doing this to help me. All this pain would someday be worth it. When you're young and looking for answers when you get hurt, there is always someone eager to tell you that the hurt you absorb is for your own good, that pain is a value added to the summation of your life. That you will be made stronger for it. How lucky we were to learn these hard and important lessons.

I still tell myself that this was worth it. I still lie to myself about the virtuousness of the lessons that have been beaten into all the parts of my body you will never see. I still brag about the scars left behind.

It took a while for Pearl Jam to really settle in for me. *Ten* and *Vs.* were inescapable records, but after Cobain's death, and as the '90s unfolded and alt rock, pop, and hip-hop started to dominate airwaves, Pearl Jam faded into the sea a little. It wasn't until their fifth record, *Yield*, that I brought them back into my life.

Yield, released in 1998, is where Pearl Jam starts to materialize as a dad rock band. Three years earlier, they had teamed with Neil Young—long considered the "godfather of grunge"—as the backing band on his album *Mirror Ball*, further rooting their feet in both past and present. Eddie Vedder often cited bands like The Who as his primary influences, and on *Yield* a broader musical landscape started to appear behind them. It's both a return to form with the righteous fury of their earlier work—tracks like "Brain of J" and "Do the Evolution" are faster, harder, and more aggressive—but there's a weariness that appears in Vedder's voice. An earlier anger felt now by older men, Vedder in his mid-thirties no longer processing the fury of youth or the exuberance of grasping at celebrity for the first time. The Pearl Jam that appears on *Yield* is a band working on a careful balance, contemplation and tenderness threading throughout all the raised voices and brash power chords. They were no less angry but finding a better use for difficult emotions as tools we cannot help but wield. Anger not something driven by fists and decibels, but exasperation and desire.

There are teeth still on *Yield*—it famously shares a connective thread in 1998 with Korn in having a Todd McFarlane animated music video for "Do the Evolution"—but the singles that played from a blown-out speaker cut into the drop ceiling at the grocery store were "Given to Fly" and "Wishlist," contemplative, soft, and tender songs that perched on a cliff that could throw sappy to schmaltz with the lightest breeze.

A wave came crashin' like a fist to the jaw,
Delivered him wings, "Hey, look at me now."

I came to understand the teeth that hid behind tenderness. Every time a man laid hands on me, I was told that this was for my own good, a lesson, a blessing. Aren't I so lucky? And every time a man laid hands on me, I retreated into myself, found all the nerves and wires carrying emotions through my body and began to sever them. Turn it all off. If you start to feel nothing, then nothing really hurts. I was a born crier who suddenly stopped and replaced it all with apathy.

I WAS ALWAYS TOLD THE YUKON was where the men were men, and the women were too. I knew what I was supposed to be, and I knew the version of myself lying in secret, this screaming pit inside me where I threw the queerest parts of my soul to hide away. I wanted to believe that I could be tender and soft and edging on sappy, and I wanted someone to show me that was possible.

But first he was stripped, and then he was stabbed,
By faceless men, well, fuckers, he still stands.

This is how the radio saves a life. Men in my life were not always or even often the best guides, but they were not the only men I had to offer guidance. On *Yield*, Eddie Vedder was trying to find his way through a youth spent in angry and brash corners and make sense of the onset of adulthood. Finding himself in his thirties and looking for softness to grant comfort, leaving behind just the lessons he had learned walking a wavering path, inviting listeners to learn from what he left behind.

Got to be something better than in the middle

"ONE HEADLIGHT"
THE WALLFLOWERS

The first time I ever remember hearing the Wallflowers, I was covered in blood, moldy produce, and garbage. When the garbage compactor jammed at Food Fair, often the only way to get it running again was to climb through the steel hallway that bridged the hollow expanse of the loading bay to the side of the garbage bin, jump into the compactor, and dislodge the bits of rotten food, expired meat, and old cardboard by hand until the compactor moved again. Once you were sure it was moving freely, you could climb back out through the steel tunnel, which was also often covered in blood and rotten food bits and liquids of unknown origin. I learned quickly to bring a change of clothes, and I never really thought about how crushing it was to be getting paid minimum wage to do this.

My dad never wanted me to follow him into working as a glazier. It's not that he was ashamed of his work; my dad has always been good at his job and proud of it, and rightly so. It's that he knew it was hard and dangerous work, and I think if you spend your life doing hard, dangerous work it can wear you down. It's not that he didn't want me to work like him; it's that he was worried about me being weighed down by the spiritual cost of hard and demanding labor. This is a common dad denominator, especially dads who work in labor, that they want something different, something that feels better, for their kids.

I never really wanted to be my dad, but I have always wanted my dad to be proud of me. I still, at the time of writing, want my dad to be proud of me. For all the days he and I share on this earth, I will want this. Not desperate for approval but desiring it all the same. I want him to feel like he did something right in raising me, teaching me, guiding me, and showing me the way. My dad is a very accomplished man in a thousand ways, and I want him to feel like I am counted in that number. Raising me was just as much work as any labor he performed with his hands.

The Wallflowers are fronted by Jakob Dylan, and you will be told immediately that Jakob is Bob Dylan's kid. I imagine being a musician named Jakob Dylan is like being in Duckburg with the last name McDuck. You can hide the facts all you want, but people are putting the clues together without you. You can hear it in his voice, the tones of his father, the Dylan-esque gravel that inspires his tongue. The influence of his dad shaping the way he finds a way through this life.

"One Headlight" was the second single from the Wallflowers' T Bone Burnett–produced second record, *Bringing Down the Horse*. The Wallflowers hadn't made much of a splash with their first album, roots rock that was fine enough but nothing truly special. Even being Bob Dylan's kid wasn't enough to make their self-titled debut take off. You have to admire Jakob for wanting to make his own way in the music industry and believing that it was on his own terms, that being the son of Bob Dylan wasn't anything particularly special. Nepotism is funny like that, an unseen force moving things around like wind shifting slowly through the trees. If you're not looking, you won't even see the leaves it jostles free from their branches. This is not to discredit the strides that Jakob and the Wallflowers made in between their debut and working on *Bringing Down the Horse*, but I'm sure it certainly helps to carry that last name through the door.

I never really understood my dad when I was young—I never understood men in general—but I looked at him as the key detail with which to understand the larger tapestry, a reference piece I could use as a guide. If I could make him proud, then men might see me as something equal. When I was a teenager working a nothing job at a nowhere grocery store, I saw in him this hardworking tradesman, up before dawn, home late tired and worn through. I started to wonder how I could find a way to emulate him without ever having to follow him into the trade I was being kept at bay from. I looked around the grocery store for the first stepping stone, thought the bakery would be a place to start. Somewhere I could learn a trade that uses my hands, that I could throw myself into, that I could get lost in.

I wanted to make my way in this world on a path I could determine, not ask my dad for help or to open doors for me. I never once thought to sit down with him, ask questions to get his thoughts or his feelings on anything. I made assumptions and drew my life around them.

At sixteen, I asked to be transferred into the bakery at Food Fair. I was going to be a baker. I was going to make my own destiny.

The first single from *Bringing Down the Horse* isn't "One Headlight," which is always a surprising fact to remember. It was "6th Avenue Heartache," a title winking at Bruce Springsteen's "Tenth Avenue Freeze-Out." For all the Dylan of Jakob's lineage, you can hear Springsteen in a lot of his work, hear him looking for guidance from the men who came before him as he worked to carve a path to claim as his own. Singles and hits get lost as time washes over our memories, and it's easy to forget that "6th Avenue Heartache" was everywhere, drive-time radio DJs cutting in with their insistent reminder that this single was from, you'll never guess, Bob Dylan's kid.

I believed that all dads were like mine. Protective, caring. Watchful. That all dads hold this one instinct, shared among their kind. Look out and guide where needed, be gentle. But all fathers are not dads, and this is a hard lesson to learn.

The bakery department at Food Fair in Whitehorse in the '90s was notorious for exactly one reason, which explained why young women didn't work there: The head baker was a lecherous man who could not let a woman exist on this earth without commenting on his perception of her body, all the things he felt women and their bodies owed him. The things he wanted to do. Women were objects for him to desire and lust after. But it was just talk, always talk. Never serious. And I was by all perceptions a boy, and I believed this made me safe.

"One Headlight" is where the Wallflowers leave their mark, a song that feels like a foot in all doors, tones of Jakob's father but shades of something more, the product of time spent honing a voice that felt like a unique watermark to leave on this earth. *Bringing Down the Horse* made a name for the band in all the ways their debut didn't, one that transcended the lead singer's last name and cemented them as something new. A Dylan for a new generation. Jakob was eternally cursed to talk about the legacy of his father by last name alone. He was a son yearning to be known as something other than the by-product of his family line.

I wanted to work in the bakery because I thought this shift in responsibilities would change something in me. This was where I would start finding my own path, discover some passion for dough and kneading that I had never known was there. It took me off the floor and gave me a taste of real responsibilities, no longer part of the common rabble stocking shelves and getting carts. I had transcended and moved into a new arena. Maybe this was how I would make my dad proud, make my own way, and leave my mark.

I had not heard "6th Avenue Heartache," or at least it hadn't registered. Despite it being ever present on the radio, it never hit me in the heart the way a song that will live in your soul forever should. We didn't have cable TV at home, and without MuchMusic (Canadian MTV) I never got to see the David Fincher–produced music video, the Wallflowers moving through a scene in still photographs turned into stop motion. A flip-book of their lives to date, building to something big. "6th Avenue Heartache" had laid the first bricks, and "One Headlight" came after to form the walls of the hearth.

It's a song that burns slow, like a match struck without need for a flame. The iconic movements that lead us into the music, sparse notes of a guitar, drums without cymbals, the hint of an organ. It's a perfect grocery store song in that it feels alive, and it feels real and tangible and human. It's easy to poke fun at or mock grocery store radio rock, but to me and my heart it always feels like home. Songs live and breathe in stores like this, contain all the breadth of their emotions played through shitty speakers hidden away in the ceiling. The music that moves around bodies as they search for something, lost in thought, walking through the world. Lives move through these spaces and are marked forever by them in unseen ways. Dust that builds on the soul to mark time. These are real and human songs that play for everyone, live in all of us, and leave us with their memories. There is, perhaps, no more alive a locale than a grocery store. A beating heart that will always be overlooked and forgotten but will form foundational memories of sound and the banal tactile sensations of the world. Feeling freshly bagged bread in your hands, the brisk chill of water as sprinklers turn on to lightly crest hills of fresh produce. The sound of squeaky wheels on freshly waxed floors, a door opening automatically via a sensor hidden above your head.

This is where I first fell in love with the way that music and the sound of the world can haunt you forever.

My first memory of hearing "One Headlight" was after crawling out of the trash compactor chute, covered in blood and expired food and garbage. Standing in a loading bay with a coworker who came along to observe for safety, lest I be crushed by the moving steel wall when it got unstuck. Another guy I worked with who had lent me two dollars the week before to buy a cheese bun and a coke for lunch came barreling in to demand that I pay him back what was owed to him. I stood there like a garbage bag that had come alive, incredulous to the immediacy of his needs and trying to just hear the song playing through the speakers. It was always a welcome change when a new song became a hit and started to enter the drive-time playlists and mix things up. New sounds to break through the old. Listening for Jakob Dylan's voice as he sang "come on try a little, nothing is forever, there's got to be something better than in the middle" until there were hands on my shirt shaking me, yelling over the music into my ears.

"Pay me my fucking money."

I am marked forever by this moment just as I am by the song. This guy whose name I've long forgotten yelling at me like a loan shark out for blood over a two-dollar debt still in its earliest stages of delinquency. Shaking the blood and expired food juice loose from my shirt. I didn't have his money, but it didn't seem to matter. He was shaking me and yelling at me, and all I wanted to do was listen to the song. Just let me disappear into it for a moment and then I'll find your money. Shaking me again and yelling, "Just pay me my fucking money; you can afford it now that you moved up to your fancy little bakery."

This was me learning I had been othered in my shifting career. That moving off the floor and into a department had changed me in the eyes of my once fellow stock boys. Even though I had been here longer than most of them now, even though it was my time to move up, to find my calling. I was still poor, still a worker, still laboring for minimum wage. I was covered in garbage and blood from the garbage bin—couldn't they see I was just like them? Was I even like them at all? I was suddenly alone, not connected to my former brethren stocking shelves and left alone in a bakery with a leering predator.

I remember asking my older sister what she wanted for Christmas, and she told me she "kind of liked that Wallflowers record," elevating the band to some cooler level than they had previously held in my heart.

My sister is two years older than me, and in our younger years was the picture of everything I wanted to be. Smart, clever, popular but never untouchably so. She was then and remains today a kind and thoughtful person, not one to be cruel or mean spirited. She is, above all, a protective and careful person. When I was bullied, which I'm sure was more than I was ever fully aware of, she made sure she was outwardly kind and there for me, that her friends looked out for me too. This all makes her sound like a political figure moving through the halls of a high school, and anyone who has ever been in proximity to high school popularity knows this is at least kind of true. I know it must have been a burden to have a younger sibling who was the polar opposite of her, quiet and weird, the target of ridicule and implied cruelties. I always wanted to be her, or at the very least get somewhere close to knowing how it must have felt to climb to the top of a social ladder.

I'm not sure my sister and I were ever close, but we have always tried to be. We didn't share deep secrets or hold marathon conversations about love and life and the fears that kept us awake. We spent time in our youth together in small ways that stayed with me for a lifetime. I think she tried, in all the ways she knew, to find a way to reach me or connect with me, and it's only that I never really knew myself that kept us at bay.

The only reason I ever watched the best romantic comedies of the '90s was because she asked whether I wanted to watch them with her, and watching movies with her on the uncomfortable pull-out sofa bed in our unfinished basement was the most I ever felt like I had a place in the world.

Analogue influencing worked best when it confirmed my own desires. I knew I liked "One Headlight," but my sister liking it too made it this tangible scrap of popularity. "One Headlight" became my song; the opening chords strummed on a guitar became a little trigger that let me know the next four minutes would be okay. The radio saved my life day by day. Working in the bakery meant that I was often alone, pushing loaves through the bread slicing machine or slathering nearly expired loaves of French bread with garlic butter out of a big tub we kept under the counter to turn them into garlic bread. Grocery store bakeries are exercises in repetition: bring frozen dough out from the freezer in the back of the store; pull frozen sticks of future bread out from boxes and put them into the proofer. Once risen, loaves go into the ovens or get formed into cheese buns.

My lasting legacy was making the cheesiest possible buns. Where my boss would sprinkle cheese on top and call it good, I journeyed the extra mile: rolled the dough in cheese, opened up the pores of the dough and found places to hide flavor. My opportunity to rebuild my connection to the workers in all the other parts of the store was in being known as the person making an art of cheese buns. I was frequently reprimanded for my commitment to the fromage experience, but I could not be deterred. I worked alone, a student trying to become a master, rolling frozen premade dough into cheese-based treasures to curry favor with the people I had left behind.

"One Headlight" is that perfect kind of radio song: a hit that plays endlessly throughout the days that contains notes for everyone to take away from it. The work would often feel soul crushing, banal, and demeaning. But if the right song came on at the right time, your day was saved, even just for four minutes.

I would stand behind the counter pushing bread into the slicer and sing along to the songs that tethered us all together loud enough so that my voice might rise over the half wall dividing the bakery from the checkout aisles on the other side in search of friendship. Singing over to comrades to signal that I was still here with them.

Come on try a little, nothing is forever.

The Dylan legacy hangs over Jakob with the Wallflowers, and it certainly lives there in the bones of his work, but "One Headlight" works as an exemplary showcase of Jakob's clear and abiding love of Bruce Springsteen. The roots of rock and roll that Springsteen himself certainly pulled from include the work of the elder Dylan, as if they conspired together as dads to raise Jakob. The love of the Boss isn't laid subtly in the work: "It's cold, feels like Independence Day" a reference to "Independence Day" and "I turn the engine, but the engine doesn't turn" to "One Step Up."

Weekends at the bakery started in the early morning, beginning my lifelong love affair with waking up at 6:00 a.m. to go to work. I think about the stereotype of the hockey dad, their lives told in heartwarming commercials, waking up early and bleary-eyed to make coffee with disheveled hair and plaid pajama pants before driving their future superstars to a rink.

Legends chasing assured destiny. My dad lived a different path, was always awake and ready to drive me to work in the ungodly hours of the day because he was always doing the same himself. On weekends he drove me to the Tim Hortons down the street from Food Fair. I had to grab three racks of donuts and drive them over to our own store, where we put them on the shelves in the bakery and sold them for thirteen cents more than the Tim Horton's sticker price.

I got along well with my boss, the head baker, because for a while he saw me as something I was not: the peacock version of myself as I strutted around in front of other men to try and show them I might be counted in their number. A survival tactic. But when he made comments about women to me, I could never follow his logic or play his game, and eventually he came to realize I wasn't like him. One morning while proofing bread before the store opened, he asked me if I was some kind of fag. A word spit with malice and bitterness. I protested half-heartedly. I liked women after all, but I also understood myself as a body constrained by a gender I did not connect with. He laughed and pointed out my flaws and failures. There was no way a little thing like me could ever satisfy a woman. I was close to being one myself, he said. Weak and timid and easily broken. Then his wife called to chat and he belittled her in cowardly little ways, and I finally saw him as a sad and broken machine playing at some former glory he only ever imagined was real.

He loved the worst music, like KISS, which is always and eternally now a red flag. Any song that came on the radio was never as good as KISS. I've always known that men who are a little too into KISS are often a little too obsessed with their perceptions of women and other men. Tend to be the type to spit words like *fag* at people they see as something other than themselves. I would disassociate and let him talk at me about KISS and Gene Simmons, just waiting for "One Headlight" to come on the in-store radio.

The chords that open the first few seconds will save your life. A slow and steady rhythm rolling in like the tide, drawing with it a mournful organ, gathering a story of riddles and half-truths to get lost in. "One Headlight" sounds like a conversation with death, as Jakob Dylan laments the loss of an old friend in the opening verse. In interviews since, he has talked about how he likes to lean on metaphors and images in his work to circumvent directly telling you what he means, but it never stops the song from being read as something much more literal. Jakob Dylan is a songwriter like his father in some ways—despite neither of the two ever speaking much about the other—playfully hiding behind poetic subterfuge to avoid a direct path through. Letting you lose yourself in the rhythms of their work instead.

All the same, the song sounds dark. Brooding and introspective but not cold or detached. There's something hopeful in here, yearning and sifting back through the past while building the truth of the present. "There's got to be something better than in the middle." It felt dark and foreboding but promising, like a transitional season slowly brushing away memories of old weather.

Fall mornings in the Yukon were quiet and crisp. There is a delicate silence to the changing season, a movement that happens swiftly. You only have to blink to miss it.

One fall morning—quiet and crisp—I arrived at work, dropped the Tim Hortons donuts on the counter to be rebranded as our own, and went to the freezer in the back to load carts full of frozen dough to fill the day's labors. Down the plywood and cardboard–lined hallway of the stockroom, I heard the head baker calling my name, yelling at and about me. The iron-tinged blood of aggression stained his voice. I walked out of the freezer to find his voice and asked what he wanted, and he yelled at me that he had been looking for me all over. When I asked him what for, he looked at me plainly, dead-eyed, and said that he was going to pin me against the wall and fuck me in the ass.

A silence. Nothing. I was a teenager becoming an adult in the void left between his comment and any further movement. I had become just another something to him, an object to leer and joke at. I said I wasn't feeling well, told him that I needed to go home, that I thought I had the flu, and then I sat outside and cried until I was nothing, walked home alone with puffy red eyes, climbed into bed, and felt numb for a very long time.

The one part of "One Headlight" Jakob Dylan has emerged to explain is the central theme, one that starts to appear in the first verse. It is about the death of ideas, that there should be a code of respect and appreciation. He was talking about the music industry at large, but the same can be extracted and placed over the lives of so many of us. I assumed that I had safety working in the bakery with this man because he was older, he was a father, he saw me as a body that wasn't his to turn into an object. But that idea was killed, broken in a moment with an offhand joke in the back hallway of a grocery store. It broke me, killed my spirit and reminded me that I existed as something else.

I had been struggling with the perception of my gender for years. Early memories of stomping around our house wearing my mom's boots and announcing the desire to be a woman out loud to anyone who could hear emerged from the mental filing cabinets where I had hidden them away. I thought if I worked with all these men in all the man areas of the grocery store that I would eventually learn how to be one too. Like when your classmate spends the summer in Australia and comes back with a somewhat convincing accent. But now it had been made clear to me that I wasn't seen as a man, I was seen as something else. Something to be preyed on, a victim in the making.

The numbness I felt became a lasting impression. I went back to work a few days later but was a little quieter, more reserved, insular. When songs came on the radio that I liked, that connected me to the world I lived in and the people working there with me, they didn't hit the same anymore. I sang along less, pretended to be someone else more. This is how nihilists are born, by giving them everything and showing them all the ways in which it will hurt and never explaining how to live with the pain.

I asked to be taken out of the bakery shortly after. Just put me anywhere, I didn't care. I wasn't trying to make anyone proud anymore, wasn't trying to prove to my dad or any other man that I could be someone if they just gave me a chance. I went inside myself and threw away all my ambitions, looked for a way to survive. Leaned into feeling nothing and accepting fate.

"One Headlight" is somber and brooding but ultimately grasping at hope. There is always a way to get by. That one headlight is often all you need to survive—nothing is forever— you only need to learn how to survive long enough that someone somewhere might heal you.

Why the hell are you so sad?

"IF IT MAKES YOU HAPPY"
SHERYL CROW

No child believes themselves to be different at first. There is no different when there is no real sense of what is considered normal. Normalcy is a construct, an idea drawn up, taught, and demonstrated. I want to say I knew I was different when I was young because I knew that when I grew up, I wanted to be a woman. But that wouldn't really be true. I didn't know at first that this would make me different. To me, for a good long time, it was a perfectly normal thought. The hope that eventually we all get to choose the gender we grow old as. Whatever I was born as seemed immaterial; I would eventually be granted the grace to choose my own destiny, live and die on my own terms.

The first time I demonstrated my desire to chase destiny, I was clomping around our house wearing my mom's old horse-riding boots. Leather knee-high ones that lived in a closet, relics of a life she lived before I was born.

I wanted to be just like her.

My boot wearing was cute, but a little queer. Different. We learn the words to describe being different well before we learn words that give shape to the truth.

Sheryl Crow scrapped her first record. It's a lost album most people will never hear, unless you're someone who finds and collects little music artifacts for conversational kindling at frigid dinner parties. Crow made an entire record we never heard, that didn't sound like the voice she wanted to have. Too poppy maybe. Too clean. Too pristine. Too someone else. This is an impossible task, to know who you are well enough that you are able to turn away from opportunity in order to hold on to it. Even at great and grave personal cost.

Crow was teaching music in an elementary school in Missouri when she got a life-changing gig singing a jingle for McDonald's. The windfall from the commercial brought in enough cash and confidence to spark the flames of desire, that she might be capable of so much more. Crow took her cash, bought a shitty car, and drove to LA, where she might be lucky enough to hold her dreams in her hand and build them into something everlasting.

I worked in a grocery store for four years, from when I was thirteen in 1995 up until age seventeen. When I first entered through the front doors with a crisp blue smock and a box cutter, I had no idea how much this early taste of labor would change me forever, mark its time on my body. I carry a scar of it on my back to this day as a reminder. On the right side of my body, just below my armpit and in the most awkward goddamn spot to itch, there's a raised portion of healed-over skin. It's the kind of alarming attachment to a body that people ask about with concerned tones the first time they see me without a shirt. I have heard that normal scars don't heal like that. But the early damage we absorb does not always leave normal scars.

Sheryl Crow started her career as a backup dancer and singer for Michael Jackson. There are facts in this world that once you learn them will never leave the files stored in your mind, and this is one of them. Sheryl Crow dancing and singing behind Michael Jackson on the *Bad* tour in 1987, her hair puffed up and sprayed into place so big and so bold that you might see it from space. It almost doesn't feel real, like someone is telling you about a world that never existed but feels so close to ours that it could almost be true. In an interview with Kevin EG Perry in *The Independent* in 2019, she recalled her opening request of Jackson as a simple and bold request: "Hi Michael, my name is Sheryl Crow and I just moved here. I'm a former music teacher and I would love to go on the road with you."

Sometimes we get what we ask for, and sometimes the thing we desire the most is the first blade to mark the skin.

I didn't have the language to describe myself. No words were freely available to me in the 1990s that felt descriptive enough. Trans people were out there, queer people were out there, but they were largely hidden, and the few who poked their heads above the parapets were intensely scrutinized. Freaks. *Queer* was a word brandished like a torch and pitchfork. Trans people were the villains or the shocking reveals in movies like *Ace Ventura: Pet Detective* or *The Crying Game*, or they were shocking reveals on Jerry Springer if you stayed home sick from school to watch daytime TV. I knew from a very young age that I didn't want to grow up to be a boy, then a man. But I lacked any ability to call myself a name that made sense. So, I hid these facts, buried them deep inside the caverns of myself where no one could find them and shut myself down to bolster the defense of their truths. I learned very early that to save myself I had to not let anyone really see me. Always play the safest role in the game I had been thrust into. That is how I would survive.

The first thing every man told me about working at Food Fair was about the cashiers. Our bosses, all of them men for the first two years I worked there, notoriously hired only women they could lust after to work as cashiers. This was a rumor confirmed to me the day that I was hired, in a closed room behind a closed door with a man my mom trusted who was offering me a job. He said that one of the perks of working there was being able to look at the cashiers. Like they were on display, or a line item in your paycheck every two weeks. "We only hire the hot ones," he told me, "for the front of the store. That's what we want people to see when they walk in." Then he winked and slid a box cutter across a counter to me.

I've never met a man who winked that I could trust.

I had no language or words to tell him, or anyone, that I wanted to work at the front of the store too. To be seen and counted in the cashier line, that my desires all led me to this one place. To feel like I belonged, and wasn't just toiling and existing.

I read a profile of Sheryl Crow in the *Guardian* in 2019 that opens with her claiming that she was never cool. It feels a little insulting as a person who has always thought she was cool, but also a little true when you look at it the right way. Isn't the truth always kind of a little painful? Crow was kind of an outlier; when she broke big on radio with the singles spiraling out of her debut record, *Tuesday Night Music Club*, she was flanked on music charts by the last Nirvana record, the Smashing Pumpkins, Björk, the Flaming Lips, PJ Harvey, and the emergence of Liz Phair. *Alt-rock* was birthed to give a name to anything that felt like it didn't fit on traditional radio or in easy genres, dissonant, angry music made by the people sold as the freaks and the weirdos. Sheryl Crow entered with tender and heart-wrenching songs rooted in music born of records found in parents' basements, the kind that emerges from an old piano in a childhood living room. Not cool as a cutting-edge marketing tool, but cool as something beautiful and everlasting.

Tuesday Night Music Club was how I got to know Sheryl Crow; I am certain it's how most people did, but there may be those who remember her first as a nameless woman in photos with Michael Jackson on a stage. A former music teacher from Missouri who got discovered and made it big, made it to this place, sharing a stage with the biggest pop star in the world. Wasn't she so lucky? There are also people who will remember her being positioned as an object of Jackson's affection in tabloids. It's a challenging life, being a woman in the music industry who is eager to leave her mark and willing to work as hard as she can to make that happen. Hard work can always be exploited, after all. There is always a man in desperate need of his own sense of control who can be there to turn the world to his favor, and it was a while before we knew that this was true of Jackson's former manager Frank Dileo.

It's easy to assume the villain in the Michael Jackson–Sheryl Crow story is going to be Jackson, since the unavoidable part of his lasting legacy is as a man embroiled in scandal and allegation. But with Crow, there was a veneer, a hastily built construct to make it appear like Jackson was falling for his beautiful new backup singer, a tabloid theory that Crow would later say was built only to make it seem like Jackson was even interested in women at all. Jackson's one-time manager Frank Dileo was the predator lurking behind the scenes of scandal and allegations. It took a long time, much longer than it should have, for Crow to describe the sexual harassment she faced from him, harassment that so many women in so many corners of the world faced and hid away and kept for themselves, scars that don't heal normally.

It took me a long time to understand what happened to me.

It might be happening as I write this.

When I was hired at Food Fair, there were rules, a carefully constructed normalcy. We understood the arenas where men deserved to be; we knew where women belonged. We knew the roles of each disparate group, separated by boundaries and tasks. Women were given the front of the store, they ran the tills, they controlled the in-store announcements and the calls to action. They were the first thing a customer saw when they walked in and the lasting impression after bags were packed and receipts were handed off. They were women that men could desire, women that wives could be angry at their husbands about. This is what we were told.

I always wanted to be just like them. But this was not in my arena; this was different, outside the boundaries of a carefully constructed normalcy. The cashiers at Food Fair were hired to be ideas of desire for indecent men, but they were so much more. They were funny, charming, smart, and capable, and the twine holding all things together. They were teenagers making enough money to go to college and get the fuck out of this place. They were friends who forgot they took a lot of acid on the same day they all had to go to work, creating a legacy in the story left behind of the three cashiers tripping balls all throughout an afternoon shift in the early summer. They were stories of lives I was desperate to live in.

I made sure to be the first to answer calls for packers (bag boys), carts, or a carry-out. Anything to live in their world for just a moment, this world of stories and legends and inside jokes. The cashier line was a little universe within itself that felt untouchable.

I don't really remember the first time I heard Sheryl Crow. It was maybe on a mixtape, the one some guy made for my sister when he was courting her in high school. Neither she nor I can even remember his name now, but he made a hell of a mixtape, and it's his own fault that he couldn't live up to the expectations that come with a perfectly sequenced collection of songs. I'm almost positive "All I Wanna Do" was on that tape, but that tape doesn't exist anymore, and who's to say it was ever even real?

I'm agnostic, but I can still firmly believe that "All I Wanna Do" is proof that God loves us and just wants us to feel alive. It wasn't the first single on *Tuesday Night Music Club*, but it was the first one that broke through and introduced us to her, and her to us. It wasn't the first single, nor was it the second; it was the third shove that knocked the Coke machine over, adapting "Fun," a poem written by Wyn Cooper in 1987, found in a book lying around the studio. Despite the words not being Crow's, it nonetheless establishes the foundation of what would come to be a natural strength of her songwriting: little pocket universes of a life told over the length of a song, snapshots of people in all the places the world might choose to not see clearly or with grace. She is surrounded by men in a dive bar, none of them perfect but all of them real. Lives given bone, skin, breath, and desire.

Tuesday Night Music Club is the kind of record that should be isolated and studied. There are secrets in here, some alchemy and raw talent that built a debut on the strength of a rich and deep commitment to creating a world to hide away in. We don't know the record that Crow scrapped before this one, but hearing this it's easy to imagine all the opposites it might have been. Maybe it leaned too much on pop that didn't feel natural, songs that didn't feel like a true extension of her voice. A voice like perfectly steeped tea, warm and smooth with a bit of a kick. Crow's work is textured, a masterpiece in a gallery that you're allowed to touch and retain the sensory memory of being so close to something so beautiful.

There is dispute about the songwriting on *Tuesday Night Music Club*, how much of it is owed to Crow and how much to the titular club of men she jammed with, developed songs and craft with, and eventually turned it all into her debut album with. Kevin Gilbert, whom Crow had been dating in the early days of the music club, would later claim that she was receiving disproportionate praise and royalties for the songs on the record. Alongside other club members like David Baerwald, he started crafting a combative narrative in the press about Crow and her contributions to the songs that started to creep up radio playlists and *Billboard* lists. There was turmoil and innuendo and aspersions cast, and it fell on Crow to make it known that her success wasn't an accident. It was deserved and earned and hers.

It was impressive that I worked up the nerve to request a transfer out of working in the bakery at Food Fair, after the head baker joked that he wanted to pin me against the wall and fuck me in the ass. I worked hard and I showed up every day, even the bad days, even the day Ryan Downing died in gym class at school and my dad, who was Ryan's and my cross-country skiing coach, drove me to work holding back tears in the bench seat of his 1988 Chevy S-10. I broke down sobbing in the bathroom. I was becoming such a fine young man. And the world was changing to accommodate fine young men like me.

The glass ceiling in the grocery store had shattered, and one of our bosses—the guy who nearly choked the life from me because my endcaps needed work—had quit, leaving a managerial vacancy. The talk around the bench seats in the break room upstairs was that it was going to be a woman. I remember people laughing that Jackie was going to be the manager. She was so little, she was too nice, she was . . . you get it. The list continues. But Jackie, a woman who had previously worked day shifts in the store, became a manager. And she wanted to make some changes.

It was Jackie who allowed me to move into the bakery in the first place, and it was Jackie whom I trusted when I talked about the head baker joking about sexually assaulting me, and it was Jackie who was the only goddamn person, this small and nice and whispered-about woman, who believed me when I said it affected me. Other men talked about how a man should be able to take a joke, but they had stopped seeing me as a man long ago, called me names and cast doubt on my manhood, and I never bothered to correct anyone when they finally got something right.

It was Jackie who saw me, I think, or saw something. A flicker of a flame hinting at desire. It was Jackie who broke the system down and rebuilt it. She asked if I would be interested in becoming a cashier. The first cashier who was, and the truth of this depends on whom you ask, a man. I said yes so goddamn fast.

The Wikipedia page for Sheryl Crow's 1996 self-titled album can barely hide its contributors' contempt for her success, going so far as to lay the blame at her feet for the suicide of John O'Brien, the man who wrote the book *Leaving Las Vegas*, from which Crow adapted the song of the same name. David Letterman asked her in 1994, in an impromptu moment on live television in the early stages of her life as a Famous Woman, if the song was autobiographical. She responded with an immediately noncommittal "sort of," which served as enough of a slight to the people who felt they were owed more by her that they could never forgive her perceived transgressions. The men of the Tuesday Night Music Club had claimed some ownership of Sheryl Crow and were upset that she had been struck by lightning and turned wholly real instead of simply being their open door to endless success.

This record is her release. Her own name, no music clubs or other people or men who are owed and expectant. Not even so much as a title to distract from making it known she was here, she was never going away, and you were going to hear from her every goddamn day.

Music held us all together like reused tape, all of us toiling away for minimum wage in a grocery store in the lower middle of upper Canada, holding on but often just barely. The radio gave our lives structure: the same songs populated the same hours on the same days. We knew every song; we knew how to sing along to what we thought the words were to beloved choruses. When a new song entered the arena, became part of the delicate ecosystem of radio, there was always the concern that this could tip the scales, upset the balance.

"If It Makes You Happy," the clear standout of Sheryl Crow's self-titled album, was not made for grocery store radios—though you could argue that all songs destined to become hits in the age of radio were made for them—but if you found yourself teetering on the edge of disaster, those opening chords, strings strummed loud and steady, announced a changing tide.

The first day I showed up to work to start my new life as a cashier, to be part of the opening scenery—the first thing a customer sees and the lasting impression—I wasn't allowed in the changing room. We changed in gendered washrooms upstairs from the loading bay, tiny-two stall bathrooms next to the break room and a broom closet. I opened the door to walk in, the way I had a thousand times before, to an onslaught of jeers and slurs and was told I wasn't allowed in there anymore. That's where the men changed, and I had given up that right. "Go over there with the women if you want to be one so fucking much."

It hits harder when the sentiment is so right for all the wrong reasons.

I changed in private, hid in the broom closet and quickly shed civilian clothes for work attire and waited to feel destiny in my hands. I sat on a bench in the break room among the white Styrofoam cups lingering with cold coffee and dead cigarettes and shielded my heart from endless accusations as to why I was working as a cashier. "That's a fucking girl's job," a man two times the size of me said. He announced everything around him as girlish nonsense or a guy thing that you wouldn't understand. I remember him getting increasingly frustrated at the presence of the Kim Stockwood song "You Jerk" on the radio. "This is fucking chick bullshit," he would protest. Sometimes you wonder where people went in their lives long after you parted. He's an alt-right influencer on Twitter.

To have a perfect work-background sing-along song, it needs a moment, an angle. A strange turn of phrase or a perfect hook. Something to hold on to like a life raft. "If It Makes You Happy" has its chorus:

If it makes you happy, it can't be that bad,
If it makes you happy, then why the hell are you so sad.

The rhyming couplets of *bad* and *sad* are each drawn out to imply their deepest meanings. You could lose yourself in playfully drawing them out when singing along, let each syllable trail behind you like the wind at your back. The track is built in tones of fading rock music played on radio stations that thrive in dusty garages and old trucks on their last legs. Like a memory that washes over you just when you thought it might be gone forever. Crow opens with her casual tone, as if she has opened a door to her porch to invite you up. She has stories to tell, she has seen some shit, but haven't we all?

Crow sounds not weary or worn, but weathered all the same. Like the years have left their mark and she is here to tell you the stories of their scars. Never defeated, but honest. There's an earnestness to Sheryl Crow, a safety to her voice. She will tell you all the stories, even the half-remembered ones and the outright lies, of times that she struggled to stay on her feet. Sadness washed out in major keys. Guitars dipped in dad rock garages, aged by the sun. Beautiful and warm, like the perfect idea of home and sanctuary. Sheryl Crow isn't cool, and maybe she was never meant to be cool. Maybe she is every dad that is aware of not being cool and being cool doesn't even fucking matter anyway. Being cool is a myth, a posture and a pose. Being cool is just a mask that we wear to survive, and not everyone needs it.

I felt big. That's how I remember my body standing behind a till for the first time. I have always felt small around men, but around women for the first time working as a cashier, I felt big. My body felt odd, out of place. I was aware of it in my surroundings and all the eyes on me. I was building an image of myself in my head: hulking, looming, all hard and angles and dangerous lines. I have always obsessed about the perception of my body—what I look like and how I read as a person—and now I was the lone body different than all the others standing behind a till. I thought about my voice and how it struggled to find weight when I worked around the men in the store, and now maybe I could let it go, let it raise to the heavens. Let it match Sheryl Crow as she let the words *bad* and *sad* hold on for a second or two more. Maybe I could let go.

You have to learn numbers. You have to learn so many goddamn numbers. Bananas were eleven. Carrots seven. Avocados three two six. Never say "three twenty-six"; it's confusing. Don't ask me why. The first time I ran a till by myself, the very first customer was a man who would normally stand tall enough to rest the bulge of his jeans right where a woman might stare at it as she slid items from the moving sidewalk delivering groceries from end to end onto the scanner. He raised his crotch to the counter as he always did, muttered "What the fuck" to himself when he saw me standing there, and called me a faggot.

I smiled, asked, "Paper or plastic?," and tried to lower the register of my voice with each word in a defensive pattern.

I was not a good cashier at first. There were so many codes for things: produce and social expectations. Three two six, seven nine one three. That's a leek, that's a cremini mushroom. That's a girl, you're a boy. Why are you working here? I thought only girls worked the counter? Are you a fucking girl? I learned that adults with faces you recognize without ever knowing the names behind them are at their worst when confronted with a young person in the workplace. I spent the first week as a cashier being laughed at, asked about my gender, called a faggot. Paper or plastic.

But I wanted this life. It made me proud, happy to be here, just glad to be on the team. When I heard a cart crash over on aisle 7, I knew it wasn't me that would have to clean it up. I just had to pick up the phone and press pound one one and say, "Cleanup on aisle 7" and then go back to waiting for a customer to come place his dick just high enough on the counter that I would know it was there.

It is hard to listen to "If It Makes You Happy" without hearing ghosts of the past whispering in its quiet moments. Crow opens with stories grounded in the places fame has taken her, the ponchos and mosquitoes of it all, alludes to thrift stores and city streets and unmitigated fame. And then, in a moment of wry irony, she breaks the fourth wall and winks at the half-truths and inferences that build a story. This isn't real; she was always making it up, at least a little, be it on Letterman's couch or on stages and in verse. There are always lies waging an eternal war on the truth. Maybe none of that really matters. What matters is she is here, she will always be here, pushing and working for what she wants.

According to songwriter/producer Jeff Trot, who worked with Crow on a number of songs over the years, including "All I Wanna Do," the song took time to find itself. It started life as a song he had half-written for another project, and Crow took it, changed words and added verses and changed the key to suit her voice. They tried it as what Trot described as a "twangy, David Lynch-esque sort of thing," a punk rock song, a country song, a menagerie of ideas trying to find form. Trying on genres like clothes until something fit just right. Crow's voice had turned raspy and wry since her debut, a little weary and a little angry and a little funny and whimsical and biting. Guitars and drums made big, boisterous noise behind her. The song was a classic and a breath of fresh air all at once, preposterously cool while being effortlessly not.

I think when people say Sheryl Crow isn't cool, it's a reaction to earnestness. She's not cool because she's not hiding so much as she's winking at the truth, letting it bleed through the curtain we are so often comfortable hiding it behind. We know who she tells us she is, and we can feel the world she tells us she lives in; it creates a stark reality that feels so real you could reach right out and touch it. Never afraid to hold the truth out in front of her for all to see, but never showing you all of it. Always just enough. It's a hard lesson to learn.

You get down, real low down,
You listen to Coltrane, derail your own train,
Well, who hasn't been there before?

I didn't really notice the words at first. I slowly grew into myself as a cashier, and the work felt nice to me. There was something thrilling about being the first "male" cashier, like a secret desire slowly revealing itself. Over time I learned the codes for things and how to count change in my head and what to do if someone did that annoying thing they claim is helpful by giving you extra change to make "the math easier" even though the computer did the calculations for me already. I got used to not changing at work anymore. They didn't let me in the boys' room, so I changed at home and then left for work in my work clothes. I didn't even care that when I tried to go into the washroom before work the men laughed at me, asked if I sat down to pee. I didn't care that men laughed at me as I walked by them in the stockroom, or called me a girl's name when they called out to me in the hallway. You can't hurt me with the words I wish were true.

But I had had a bad day. I had to iron my shirt at home, quickly, after school and before work, and I was already running late because a kid on the soccer field snuck up behind me while I was reading a dog-eared copy of *The Tommyknockers*—headphones on, shut out to the world—and gave me a wedgie so violent it made me bleed. I could just hear laughter, someone calling me a fag, someone calling me the girl's name that had been found to mock me.

I yelled out in pain and rolled on the grass for a moment before rushing home through the woods behind our high school, careful not to let anyone see I was crying. Always be strong. Rushed into the basement and grabbed my white oxford work shirt, put it on the ironing board with a paisley cover in the basement, smoothed all the creases and failures in the delicate cotton, and prayed the blood would stop running down the back of my leg. I leaned over to pull the chord out from the wall and my bare back touched the iron for just long enough to sear my skin like bargain bin steak, and that's where the scar on the passenger side of my back just below my armpit comes from.

I went to work, and one of the men who worked the floor could see that blood was staining the back of my pants, asked me if it was my time of the month, and I just didn't have anything left in me anymore. I told Jackie that the experiment had failed, that I wasn't working out, just put me back out on the floor where I belong. Let me change in the changing room again. I wasn't able to make myself real in the version of the world I wanted people to see. She protested only once, said that it seemed like it was going great on her end, that I had been so excited to have this opportunity. But I had been broken, and I just felt nothing where possibility had once lived.

Then why the hell are you so sad.

Being different is an idea beat and burned into your skin. I went back to working the floor at the grocery store, but I had given up. I could do my job well, but I didn't care. I began to intentionally throw fire at the problem, not willing to commit to the process of the work anymore. I gave up, became nothing, disassociating in the dairy cooler and shuffling through turning all the cans in aisle 2 so the English language side faced out. As soon as I made it clear I had given up, the men welcomed me back into the boys' changing room. Lauded as a return to form, back where I belonged, back where we don't care.

I infamously started a competition to see who could take the longest fifteen-minute break, winning when I got busted by one of our bosses coming downstairs at the three-and-a-half-hour mark. He was a youth minister at the

Baptist church my friend Tim went to. I am tormented by the memory of him cornering me in the stockroom, lowering his voice so no one could hear his seething rage as he hissed, "You're a fucking piece of shit" to me before shoving me gently against the wall.

I quit three months later.

I missed it, for a long time. I missed the energy of that store, the smell of the floor after it had been cleaned, bleach and lemon and dirt. The sound of carts crashing into each other and the wet cardboard and moldy food smell of the loading bay. The radio. Singing Sheryl Crow songs with comrades when the days became long and trying. The possible future I dreamed could become real if I found the right place to work, the right way to stand and be seen. It's not that it wasn't making me happy; it's that it had been eating away at me, and I had put my time in to this place and now it was time for me to move on and find where my name might grow into its own somewhere beyond all this. I had learned I was different, and it was time to find where different might belong.

If I could be who you wanted, all the time

"FAKE PLASTIC TREES"
RADIOHEAD

I have always lied to get what I need. Lied and stretched the truth or conjured alternate facts to shield me from harm. When I started doing poorly in school, I tried to lie and make excuses for my own lack of ambition, explain away the slipping teeth in the gears of the engine that drove my attention span. I always knew something was off-center with me: I didn't feel the way I assumed most people felt. I was always uncomfortable in my skin and my clothes and obsessed with the ways I stood and talked that might make me stand out as queer. Queer as in different. Less than.

I became obsessed with my desire to be perceived as the same as everyone else. It felt increasingly like I was the only person who stood out as starkly different, although this might have been the anxiety talking and it's just that no one thought to talk to me about anxiety when it started to appear. I was starting to fail and to collapse into myself like a dying star. I retreated into my own spaces, my bedroom in the unfinished basement of our house with a well-worn PlayStation, a translucent green Nintendo 64, and a collection of CDs growing like rhubarb in the dark. I slipped easily into digital realms and music because I could find myself in CDs with less effort than I could as a physical object in a world that felt too demanding. When all things became overwhelming or too much to bear, I needed only a pair of headphones and a quiet corner to calm me, a habit I picked up from my dad without ever connecting the dots.

Emulating the actions of my dad for a lifetime without ever once realizing it, on sunny weekends with nothing else to do I would lie down with a dog-eared copy of a Stephen King book, slip headphones over my ears to drown out all things, and work through a stack of CDs next to me, wearing out the repeat button when the right moment in the right song demanded one more spin. I have been addicted to many obsessive delights in my life. The warning signs were always there: needing everything to be exactly right there when I desperately needed to feel something despite diminishing returns. Addiction to calm the screaming parts of my brain that never turned off.

Compilation CDs were perfect for a kid with undiagnosed ADHD, anxiety, and depression. I was neurodivergent without the words to describe it. A comp CD gave me a landscape to move between worlds, and in Canada we had the perfect portal in a series of comps released by MuchMusic: Big Shiny Tunes.

The first Big Shiny Tunes was released in 1996; its track list runs through a collection of darlings of alt-rock top 10 countdowns, bands like Better than Ezra, Sloan, Foo Fighters, Fun Lovin' Criminals, and Beck. A bounty of hits that allowed curious minds to find new favorites, Big Shiny Tunes was my introduction to Radiohead. Wedged between "Ophelia" by Vancouver alt-rock band Moist and "Angry Johnny" by Poe lived "Just."

"Just," from Radiohead's sophomore record *The Bends*, was like hearing the answer to a question you had never thought to ask aloud. Frantic and paranoid and calm all at once, the soundtrack to the waves of a panic attack. Britpop was just starting to take hold in 1995, when Oasis released *Definitely, Maybe*. It became a schoolyard hit: the girls who sat out on the lawn smoking cigarettes together at recess sang "Wonderwall" in unison as they passed a half pack of stolen Player's Lights around their perfect circle.

I had a budding interest in Britpop; Oasis felt like a modern shade of the Waterboys album I could hear emerging from my dad's headphones. I knew very little about my dad, but I knew he was from Wales and Britpop felt like an entry into understanding a home he had left behind. The post-Cobain alt-rock landscape felt like it was searching for something with an angry blade clutched in its hand, but the landfall of British pop music—bands like Oasis and Suede and Elastica—felt like something more adult, weary, and tangible. It felt like my dad's hands somehow, gritty and worn and real.

Hearing "Just" for the first time produced an instant obsession, the opening strums ringing hollow and repeating until fuzzed out power chords take off like a chainsaw. It's a song that surges with anxious aggression and then pulls way back into itself, frantic and unsure of its own explosive potential. Thom Yorke's voice stays steady at the center, like he had somehow found control of a car spinning out on an icy highway. It felt like the promise hiding in all my own fears, what was possible with the synapses firing in my own brain. I spent hours with it, hitting replay again and again until the button gave out. Just one more hit. We didn't have cable at home, and I lived entirely unaware of the music video until it became an unescapable object of endless debate. Kids whispering in hallways and computer labs between Apple IIs about what they thought the whisper at the end was. A secret to plague us, open to endless speculation with zero answers. Everyone claiming a meaning for themselves in it. Children posturing as adults claiming to understand the worldview of a pop song.

Hearing "Just" led to an easy purchase of *The Bends* from the music store in the corner of the Hougen Centre, a building towering over all of Main Street, named by and for the family that owned far too much of downtown Whitehorse. I've never known how true this fact really was; it was something my mom told me that felt more real with each repeated anecdote. I learned early on to never trust people who hoarded land and property to put their names on buildings.

Every city has a Main Street, either by name or definition, a thoroughfare that divides and centers a place, and Whitehorse is no exception. Main Street runs the length of Fifth Avenue right down to the banks of the Yukon River, littered along the way with legal offices, banks, hotels, bars, and buildings that used to be bars. Fourth and Main used to host the Taku Hotel, a hotel above a beloved dive bar with a perfect nighthawk diner right around the corner. Main Street is the only street in Whitehorse I am certain about the name of; all the others are roads that connect via directions and old landmarks. Drive straight, past where the liquor store used to be, take a left by the old Northwestel building.

Whitehorse is a small town made big by the familiarity of its past to all the people whose lives have been impacted by the changes on its streets.

The Hougen Centre on Main Street is what passed for a mall in the Yukon, a two-story building that was less a mall and more a collection of small shops under the same roof. Walk through the main doors off Main Street and you would find the photo shop on your right, then the sports store owned by one of the many Hougen children who claimed stores for themselves to act like entrepreneurs, working jobs handed to them in a building with their familial name over the door. In the center of the foyer was the lotto booth operated by a man we all called Bubba, a beloved and well-known character whose real name seemed less important than the one he had chosen. Catch Bubba on the right day and he would sell you a pack of smokes without ID, or scratch cards to budding gambling addicts drawn in by the half dozen ice cream flavors sold at his kiosk. To the left of him was the gift shop my sister worked at during holidays and busy seasons, made famous by the large taxidermy in the corner: an albino moose that wore a red hat at Christmastime. Follow the hallway and you would find the lone recognizable chain store, a Radio Shack, just before the ramp leading up to the electronics and music store owned by yet another branch of the Hougen family tree. Upstairs was a shoe store, some offices, and a few stores my mom worked in at one time or another—a short-lived toy store, then a women's clothing store called Season's Fashions. She left those jobs to work at Coast Mountain Sports on the other side of Main Street, a small outdoor supply shop housed in a building made to look like the inside of a trapper's cabin.

The heart of the Hougen Centre for me was the shop where I bought my first work outfit: a white Oxford shirt and black Dockers with no pleats in the front. It was the ironically named Men's World. This is where I fled after quitting my life of grocery store labor.

I was back-to-school shopping with my mom as I prepared to enter my final year of high school in the fall of 1999, scanning walls of perfectly folded Levi's 501s, packs of Hanes Beefy Ts, and Point Zero button-down shirts. Shopping with my mom, who knew everyone in every room, was never a swift experience; it was something you had to prepare to lose hours of your life to. Conversations I would trade anything to remember now that felt so benign as they unfurled around me. I had learned to lie here, too, learned to pretend I knew and cared about the cut of men's clothing, the way they told a story on the body of a man. Derek, the store manager, asked me questions about clothes and taste and preference, and I talked through it with the perfect cadence of an expert liar.

I didn't see the changes coming until I was asked when I could start. I had no idea I had applied for a job, but I had been hired all the same, and as I stammered my way through telling Derek when my last shift at Food Fair was, he put me on the calendar of Men's World for the following weekend.

I was told to bring my personality with me to work. He showed me the stereo sitting atop a rack of clothes and said I should bring some of my own CDs with me too. Create an atmosphere with my discerning tastes.

At school and with my punk rock friends, my musical tastes all appeared to be in a single lane. We talked about

NOFX records, threw fists and shoulders at each other as we slammed the full force of our aggression against ourselves. I never let *anyone* know, let alone the other judgmental teenage punk rock kids, the full run of my taste in music. At home and in private my collection was vast and varied, the by-product of working from a young age and pouring all my available money into my obsessions. I had a flimsy shelf collapsing under the weight of thousands of CDs, but I couldn't imagine what I might bring with me to sell men's fashion. I didn't know men's fashion. I didn't even know if I was really a man at all.

I didn't bring music into the store the first day I worked at Men's World, but I drove to work that Saturday morning listening to Radiohead in the 1995 Mazda Protege my mom, sister, and I all shared. A blue sedan with a black bumper that was mostly black duct tape on the driver's side, from a cold winter morning when my mom backed into my dad's truck in the driveway by mistake and the plastic bumper shattered from the combined effects of the bitter cold and the hard steel bumper of a Chevy.

I drove to work listening to Radiohead as the lingering darkness hung low in the air. By now it was October, and in October in the Yukon the dark starts to replace the light and all things turn colder and sharper and harder. The tourists leave town, and all that is left are locals who don't know the names of any streets they travel on but could tell you how to get anywhere you could imagine as long as you knew your history.

Sitting in my car listening to *The Bends* in the cold, dark morning, sipping the final dregs of perfectly terrible coffee from the machine at the gas station next to the old KFC, "Fake

Plastic Trees" filling the void in the car as I sat, I smoked a secret cigarette and talked myself into the lie I was about to walk into.

It wears her out.

I felt tired already, not just because it was early in the morning and I had planned too generously for arriving ahead of time, leaving me with a half hour to kill in an empty parking lot in an empty city, but tired of upholding lie after lie. Cheating and tricking everyone, most of all myself. I was about to leave high school and had only just started to make friends, punk rock kids I bonded with because of our shared loved of Fat Wreck Chords bands built from power chords and simple rhythms. I worried I had lied to them too. I never let them see the real me, the me sitting in this car smoking cigarettes when I knew no one would see me, listening to Radiohead and feeling like I was building a lie that I could not maintain forever.

When I was younger, I developed an internal paranoia that my whole life was a false front. That the kids who were nice to me and the people who toned down their approach to mocking me had been paid for their time. For a few years I was certain it was my mom who had done this, and I searched for clues that might lead me to the truth when she wasn't around. It was a creeping paranoia that festered from an unknown source that would not be diagnosed until someday far in the future. The fear of not knowing yourself well enough to trust your instincts or the world around you and so you learn to question everything and everyone.

When I was a younger teen, I developed very few friends. First Tommy, who moved away with his family to Alberta when we were twelve. Then Tim, who lived kitty-corner to our house and caused worry in my heart that we were friends of convenience more than connective tissue. Then Lucas, who lived up the street from us and, of the few kids I knew, was the only one who was from a Sega Genesis house. Lucas who listened to Queen and introduced new music into my life, taught me how to play Dungeons and Dragons and DOOM on his dad's computer. Lucas who invited me to sleep over for late-night movie marathons in the corner of his living room on a pull-out couch. Lucas who just the one time propositioned me and made moves on my body I couldn't understand or say yes or no to.

In my memory, I told my mom the next day that he had tried to do this to me, and she told me it was fine, that I just wouldn't hang out with him anymore. My paranoia raised once more, conspired against reality to question who the actors working behind the scenes were that might sweep this all under the rug. A few months later it was like it all had never happened. Lucas and I hung out again, he never made moves on me, and I questioned what was real and what wasn't. Maybe I was the one was who was fake after all.

"Fake Plastic Trees" is a careful warning of the brash and unrelenting marketing upon our bodies, written by Thom Yorke in a breakdown as the band desperately tried to move away from the shadow of "Creep," the breakthrough single from their 1993 album *Pablo Honey*. It is the kind of single that fans come to hear and then leave when they don't recognize the chords and verses of other work. Yorke described writing "Fake Plastic Trees" under duress in a profile in *Blender* magazine from 2003. He said, "I spent the first five or six hours at the studio just throwing a wobbly. I shouted at everyone, and then John Leckie sent everybody else away. He sat me down, and I did a guide vocal of 'Fake Plastic Trees.'"

Jonny Greenwood claims that they had the song in three takes, and when it was finished Yorke wept.

That morning, I sat in my car, listened to "Fake Plastic Trees," listened to Yorke sing about the falseness of the world, the artifice of life, the polystyrene of it all, prepared myself for the lies I was about to live, and considered just how fake I would have to be in order for this to work. This was Men's World, and I was expected to fit the part.

My first day of work I tried to dress fashionably without knowing what fashionable was at all. I had to look it and sell it. I wore blue jeans, baggy in the leg but fitted at the waist, and an oversized yellow and brown horizontal-striped T-shirt, and white skateboard shoes. My hair was perfectly gelled into shard points. Like an older Dennis the Menace unable to let go of the lifestyle.

I walked into work that first day, said hi to Richard, the owner of both our store and the shoe store a floor above us, who most days was hidden away in an office somewhere conducting business to God knows what detail. Richard was imposing, tall and strong with a firm handshake despite two missing fingers from a wood-chopping incident in the halcyon days of his youth. You will shake a lot of hands in the Yukon, and you will become comfortable rather quickly with the frequency with which digits are missing. Richard, like many tall men in the Yukon, terrified me for only a minute before he disarmed me with a joke and a booming laugh and a rough-hewn gentleness caged in his towering frame.

Richard took a single glance at my outfit and decided to be critical without outright cruelty, telling me that generally when we work in the store, we should be wearing clothes that we sell in order to look like we work here. With a devious smile and a gentle laugh, he added, "And not look like we're just here to shoplift."

The first thing Derek taught me about retail was what he called the Zone. The presence of our bodies in relative proximity to others, always being near and close by and on call for someone's needs or desires. Providing alternate sizes, cuts, and colors and helping guide them to a purchase. It was never about the individual but rather about the cash register. Sell them what they need; turn them into their perfect form. Help guide them into a new life, one of Dockers and Levi's and expensive oversized leather jackets.

Derek was perfect in this role, the kind of man who could throw an outfit together from items he found lying on the floor and manage to make it work. Everything fit him just so, with his perfectly tidy haircut and the hint of yesterday's beard trimmed expertly on his face. Derek wore a cologne he didn't buy in Whitehorse; the whiff of something beyond all this followed him wherever he went. I knew Derek was gay, but he never talked about being gay to me or anyone, a common theme in a small town with no gay bars or cafés or specialty book shops with rainbow banners on the marquee. Whitehorse was a small, isolated town nestled in the middle of the lower end of nowhere up in the frozen parts of Canada, and above all else, the Yukon was about survival. Being queer was something that didn't survive well without the right protection.

I grew up seeing queerness on display only through easy stereotypes played for laughs on TV. I have memories of sneaking downstairs at night to turn the TV on, pushing the power button as softly as I could and swiftly turning the volume low enough so only I could hear in order to watch *The Kids in the Hall*, timing it just right to catch the opening theme by Shadowy Men on a Shadowy Planet, watching these men from Toronto—the biggest city in the country, which felt terrifying and imposing to a kid hiding in their basement in the Yukon watching the CBC on TV, tuned into the rest of the country with their dad's makeshift rabbit ears sticking out of the television. In Toronto there seemed to be a fluidity to gender and sexuality. While Scott Thompson was the obviously gay cast member, I became obsessed from a young age with the rest of the cast's willingness to lose themselves in the roles that were needed of them to fill a moment. Donning the casual drag of the workplace to act as secretaries for just a moment, because this was what was demanded of them.

I didn't see queerness on display around me in Whitehorse because for most people it was simply unsafe to let it out. That was a Toronto thing. That's a city thing. Those faggots. The Yukon of my youth was a beautiful landscape, endless mountains and rivers and vistas to stun the hardest of souls, and it was soiled only by the defensive bigotry of a small and isolated place looking to shore up its barriers from outside influences. City people brought change. City people brought queers and people of color and the kinds of bodies gruff men who staked their lives in this place used endless slurs to describe.

There was a slow afternoon on a cold weekend when Derek and I in our respective zones were helping the few customers that braved the harsh wind blowing down Main Street. Derek moved with the elegant grace of someone confident and assured in his actions, measuring bodies for suits they were certain to never wear. Inseam and out, arms and chest. While he did so, a man came up to me and asked if I could measure him the same. I told him that Derek was better at it than I was, so he would have to wait, and he told me, with words carefully chosen, that if that faggot put hands on him, he would kill him where he stood.

I have never measured anything as carefully as I did that man's inseam that day.

I wasn't selling fashion at Men's World; I was pushing artifice. The idea of a man packed and sold with a 200 percent markup. Men in the Yukon weren't the best or most adept at fashion because they were all in their own way performing some kind of drag, performing gender for an audience uninterested in their peacock feathers.

"FAKE PLASTIC TREES" IS YORKE SINGING about the artifice of the world as he saw it, driven by his desire to be something more than just the guy in the band who sings "Creep," the single that had come to define the band despite their desires to move past it and find themselves. Yorke, like so many young men, was failed by the perception of his body and his potential, failed by the desperate need to properly categorize him. Like the 1980s and all the decades before it, capitalism in the '90s sought to sell the idea of a generation back to it. The people became the product.

In the music video, Yorke sits in a shopping cart moving slowly down the aisles of a surreal grocery store, the shelves perfectly color coded in the shades of the '90s, intense greens and reds, yellows and purples. Yorke is so young here, young but already tired and fighting against a world he couldn't exert any control over. The through line connecting all things was

Yorke trying to find peace with himself. In "Creep" he pines for a perfect body because he wants to be desirable to someone else, an angel and a vision in contrast to his own perceived failures and broken spirit. "Creep" is the sound of a thousand men screaming at women about why they wouldn't like them anyway because they're weird. It hints at a scrap of self-reflection. I don't belong here.

On *The Bends*, Yorke wanted to move beyond the easy sentiments of *Pablo Honey*. The members of Radiohead—Thom Yorke, Jonny Greenwood, Colin Greenwood, Ed O'Brien, and Philip Selway—were older and worn weary from time on the road, the arrested development of youth as a moving performance of angst. The Radiohead on *Pablo Honey* didn't feel real, but it felt familiar. It felt like people I knew in passing, jocks in the hallways of a shitty high school who become half-drunk philosophers after a single can of stolen Budweiser. But on *The Bends*, Radiohead starts to feel more tangible, in part because they were breaking down just a little; Yorke was freaking out in the studio writing songs about abject anxiety and the weight of the world as it slowly pushed down on his slender shoulders. Who wouldn't snap under all that, and in snapping they made something beautiful.

I never really got comfortable in Men's World, as I never became comfortable in any man's world. Over days and weeks that became long months, I was the employee people whispered about when I was out of the room. Why was I even there at all? I wasn't particularly fashionable, nor a motivated salesperson for people looking for answers to themselves. The burning need when you cross the threshold into any fashion outlet is to know "Who will I be when I leave?" I could never answer, but I always wanted someone to tell me.

In the coldest months of winter, my job changed to something closer to punishment branded as a matter of importance. The Yukon in the late '90s was a cultural hotspot for foreign tourists, and we serviced the clothing needs of a large touring company that hosted travelers from Germany and Japan. We didn't sell them fashion, no Levi's or Point Zero or ModTimes rave pants. Richard, with his infinite business acumen, had a side hustle renting snow pants, warm jackets, and heavy winter boots to tourists, and our job was to spray them with Febreze in a small unventilated room in the basement.

If I ever wondered whether I was a good salesperson, the answer became clear when I was told my job was being temporarily reassigned to spraying Febreze into rental clothes in the basement.

I worked with one other person in our little converted office space, piles of pants and jackets and boots and no window or fan to speak of. We blasted endless bottles of Febreze into the unfiltered air, filling the room and our lungs, and played records. My coworker talked about how she thought that Common Rider was the better follow-up to Operation Ivy than Rancid. We became obsessed with the song "Infected" from Bad Religion's *Stranger than Fiction*. Maybe I just didn't belong on the sales floor. Maybe I belonged down here in the windowless basement huffing Febreze and singing "don't want to exist, I can't persist" for the millionth time in a row.

On the sales floor we were encouraged to play our own music. Derek had bought a little faux-wood CD/cassette stereo with detachable speakers, and it became our task to cultivate a vibe through its tiny output. Just play the hits, but make it your own. Derek was singularly obsessed with Macy Gray's

"I Try," and like a half-drunk DJ riding the high of a perfect evening, would often play it three or four times a shift. When he could see that it was particularly grating to me, he would sing it to me while I folded T-shirts into perfect little squares.

I could fold shirts perfectly, jeans tight and neat. Knew how to measure a man for a suit, size him for a leather jacket that would fit him just right, tight enough in the shoulders that it didn't bulge when his arms moved. I learned the movements of a man but could not emulate them. In the spring, the store expanded, opening a new space to fill with clothes and desperate for youth to market them to. Derek went to fashion shows for mid-tier retailers and came back high on the possibility of ModTimes as rave culture moved into malls. He told me we were going to try to become edgier, more raw. More real. "You're a punk rocker, right? Lean into that. Lean into yourself," Derek said.

I had nowhere to lean.

Sales always seemed slow, but this might have always been a "me" problem. To shock and entice patrons, Derek gave me thirty-five dollars in petty cash and told me to go buy some sex dolls to use as mannequins from the San Francisco store in the other mall across town, the one across from the old Canadian Tire. The Qwanlin Centre Mall, which boasted fourteen stores on the sign despite only having seven stores in reality. We were all lying about something.

Fake plastic bodies dangling from fishing line from the drop ceiling of a building pretending to be a mall, hung by my hands, pretending to be capable and connected to a body pretending to be real. The sex dolls weren't functional in the classic sense, just the plastic idea of a body that came across as more desperate than alluring. They drew very few crowds.

A theme emerges.

I wasn't really the draw my bosses wanted me to be. In the summer, sales weren't as big of a concern. Most of our money came from American tourists driving through toward Alaska, preparing to board cruise ships, who wanted to bring souvenirs with them. As we sold the idea of a comical commitment to masculinity, we also had a humidor with a selection of cigars, most notably boxes of expensive Cuban brands, which I learned were one of our bigger money makers due to a simple scheme. We sold two boxes to Americans, a box of Cubans and a cheaper box of another kind that didn't cause problems at the border, and then we showed Americans how to swap the rings in order to smuggle the Cubans across the border disguised as anything but.

Outside of this particular scheme, I wasn't much in the way of a salesman, or a man, or any of these things I was desperate to prove I could be. Derek took me aside one day and told me that when he hired me, he thought I was popular and I knew how to dress myself well, and the fact that neither of those things had proven to be true was heartbreaking to him. I was warned the ice I stood on was becoming perilously thin.

The Bends finds Radiohead at an uneasy crossroads, looking for a path to follow. Paranoid and anxious, depression moved Yorke's hand through words that battled the demons plaguing him. "Fake Plastic Trees" was a yearning plea to break through this malaise into something truly beautiful, a body that feels real in the face of so much plastic.

But it wears him out.

Being warned my job was on the line due to my general failure to present properly as a man clung to the anxious center of my heart, that I had failed so spectacularly as the kind of man I thought I was supposed to be. I wanted to be something so perfect, so good and so pure and so beautiful. But maybe this was all artifice anyway, no more real than the bargain store sex dolls hanging from a water-stained drop ceiling. I was never going to be the right kind of man in this place, and in desperation my dad asked if I would rather sweep floors at his glass shop. I could have sprinted to the quitting line. I remember when I quit, Derek said, "Probably a good call."

Hard to be mad at the truth.

I thought I could lie and cheat my way through this. I thought this was what sales were; I thought this was my one skill. The subtle subterfuge of a life. This plastic thing. Radiohead made sense to me because it was all fake. We were all broken and sad and alone and unable to see ourselves in place in the world, tormented by its mysteries and terrified of its stark realities. "Fake Plastic Trees," more than anything, is about the urgent need to be seen and validated in the eyes of those you want to perceive you, and the bitter acquiescing to a life of simple failures when it doesn't come true. Giving up, going along.

See you in heaven if you make the list

"MAN ON THE MOON"

R.E.M.

In late June 1982 in a hospital in British Columbia, a nurse washed my newborn body in a basin under running water. She was, I'm certain, a lovely and kind and caring woman who loved her job most days but probably not all days, and I imagine every now and then she circled listings in the classifieds and wondered if she should get back into retail. Some days being a nurse must be exhausting and draining, and you do what you can to get through the work. Our days are not always perfect; we survive by learning to balance difficult memories with cherished ones.

The day I was born might have been a hard day. Whatever happened, she was there but not fully present in her work, and when she was cleaning me the water—meant to wash my newly delivered body in her hands—was running directly onto my face, covering my mouth and my nose and my eyes that had only just seen fluorescent lights and tile floors for the first time. I was drowning, and she was absent in attention while my mother fought exhaustion to raise her voice loud enough to say that I was looking a little blue.

Memories linger with open-ended questions. Maybe this is just my anxiety speaking, but I am preoccupied with all the what-ifs and maybes left behind as I age deeper into adulthood. This is an idea that floats to the surface of "Drive," the opening song and central thesis for R.E.M.'s 1992 masterwork *Automatic for the People*, an album exploring nostalgia, trauma, loss, and moving forward all at once. An album about youth as it transitions to adulthood and what it means to carry the past with you into the future. Stories and half-truths that define a life. Lessons passed back from those who have managed to survive into the future of this world.

I don't remember everything, and this is the most damning thing you can say in a collection of words rebuilding your own past. Some of it just isn't there anymore. Some memories that were once a clear picture are faded images on a page, turned ashen grey with time. Some memories are just told back to me by those who only half remember ever being there themselves. Some memories are just stories to tell.

Evan Dando said it perfectly: "I've never been too good with names, but I remember faces." A woman I dated in 2002 in Alberta who drove a Jetta and was obsessed with the burned CD she had with a bootleg of the first Maroon 5 album, a guy I worked with for eight months on a high-rise building, my supervisor who was divorced and wore the same sweater every single day. I remember them, but only just, their outlines and textures. Blurry faces and voices dancing in the wind of my mind. I remember how it hurt to be dumped over text by the woman with the Jetta. I remember that supervisor showing me how to play Golden Tee at a dive bar after we left the site early because of a bomb threat.

I didn't die when that nurse nearly drowned me in a hospital in British Columbia, but water imprinted on me that day all the same, marked me with the terror of its sinister promise, and a phobia grew in me like an unchecked weed. I have always been afraid of the water, and I have always been afraid to die, and I have always been drawn to both.

When I was a kid, my mom would bathe me in the yellow and amber plaster tub in the old bathroom of my childhood home, and I would freak out every single time. Sitting in the water was fine, but when she washed my hair and the water had to run down my head and over my face, I would respond with cacophonous panic, screaming loud enough to shake the gold and yellow and brown tiles on the wall.

The neighbors called the cops more than once; they were worried something unspeakable and terrible was hiding in the darkness of our home, and it took a few times for all parties to learn that this was just what bath time was going to be like for a while. Eventually my mom got me a little shield, a green plastic and foam visor that stopped water from going over my face, and it helped bath time become something close to bearable, or at least quieter.

I don't remember any of this, but I've been told the stories, and the truth of stories told doesn't always matter as much as the dots they might connect to bridge lives together.

R.E.M. is a band of memories strung into a lifeline. Formed in 1980 in Athens, Georgia, by Bill Berry (drums), Peter Buck (guitar), Mike Mills (bass), and Michael Stipe (vocals), R.E.M.

is the progenitor of what we would start to classify as alternative rock. Everything needs a label, a genre, a category. How to classify that which doesn't work in the mainstream, until the point that it does.

In the 1980s R.E.M. didn't easily fit onto commercial streams, but they were rising steadily in popularity all the same. How do you define something that is beloved but markedly different?

R.E.M. was already popular by the time they entered my life. "Losing My Religion," from 1991's *Out of Time*, was in steady rotation on radio stations and MuchMusic. I loved them because Kurt Cobain loved them; he talked about them in magazines alongside bands like the Pixies as important to his own growth, and I was just the right age to absorb everything he passed on like a sacred truth. The prevailing rumor is that when he killed himself in a garden shed in 1995, he was listening to *Automatic for the People*. I bought a copy to help decipher the clues left behind in his wake. This was the last thing he wanted to hear before he left this world—what secrets are held in here?

I don't remember being kicked out of swimming lessons as a child, but I know it happened. I know I stalled out at earning my blue badge, when you had to be able to put your head under the water with your eyes open, at the old Lions Pool down on Fourth Avenue right next to the High Country Inn. The rub was that you weren't allowed to wear goggles, and I simply couldn't do it. I was being tested on how adept I was at managing my trauma and I failed. I became good at failing but not always good at managing it.

My mom protested to the swimming instructor that I should be allowed to move on, that I had put my whole head under water but just kept my goggles on. "That isn't good enough" is all she was told. I had to do it the same as everyone else or I couldn't move on—find and follow the mainstream. My mom was told I would never get past the point I was frozen in and that she should just take me out of class. Give up on swimming. There was no getting better than this.

R.E.M. initially wanted to make a heavier record after the release of *Out of Time*, a mostly somber and soft record that found the band moving from cult favorite status to undeniable popularity driven by the success of "Losing My Religion." I would imagine it's hard to know where to go after you achieve success previously thought unattainable. How to hold on to your voice knowing that more people than ever will hear it? It was Peter Buck who suggested they explore something a bit more reflective and slowed down. With all eyes on them, they turned pensive, pulled out mandolins and pianos, and burrowed into their origins. Trading in influences of the past and looking at the struggle of young lives as they turn old.

Automatic for the People is a masterwork of lush arrangements, alluring chords and rhythms that lay a foundation for Stipe's voice to build mazes of indecipherable poetry upon. A record of secrets, dead ends, and doubling back. Spend your life within its walls and you may never unlock all of its tightly held secrets. What is clear from the outset, as "Drive" comes slowly into focus, is that we are here to grapple with the weight of getting older. We must make peace with loss and trauma and difficult memories we can't shake. "Drive" is both first communion and last rites, the sound of a tether between worlds. Leave youth behind but remember all the scars it leaves on the body.

For many years after I failed swimming lessons, I refused to go anywhere near a pool. I never liked being underwater, didn't like how the water clung to my skin and held tight on my anxieties. I didn't like the sensation of water, and I didn't like the feeling of being exposed to the world. I also did not like the changing room.

Men change in the men's changing room.

I didn't like my body, a slow-rolling stone gathering far too much moss. I never went back to the public swimming pool, but there was a hot spring just outside of the city with an arcade in the lobby that had the Teenage Mutant Ninja Turtles game where four people could play at once, and that was enough to get me close to my greatest fear. To go into the pool, you had to first go into the changing room.

Men changed in there without any sense of fear or shame. Chests laid bare, asses and dicks hanging out for all to see. All shapes and sizes, hard angles and soft lines. As a young teenager I was growing and changing, shifting in my body and seeing the new limits it would find for itself. I'm told the first time I ever went into the changing room at the hot springs I cried and refused to get out of the bathroom stall. This, too, is a memory I don't have; it's just a story, the tale of a life half remembered.

R.E.M.'s lyrics have never traded in clarity at the best of times, and on *Automatic for the People* they only became more inscrutable. Michael Stipe's poetic twists and turns of phrase are not here to lead us down a well-worn path. Rather, he invites the listener to sift through and find answers where you need them.

Automatic leaves itself intentionally vague. Where "Drive" is the central thesis of the record, it's "Man on the Moon" that holds it together. On the surface a loving ode to deceased comedian Andy Kaufman, it's a song that fills the void between choruses with references to the Game of Life,

Mott the Hoople, and the horrible asp that plagued Egypt (it's widely rumored that Cleopatra committed suicide by sneaking a venomous asp into her chambers in a basket of figs and letting it bite her). Stipe, in an interview, stated that the repeated use of "yeah yeah yeah yeah" is because he was delighted at how often Cobain used the word *yeah* in Nirvana songs and wanted to see if he could outdo him in a single track.

There were rumors, always rumors, about Michael Stipe's sexuality. In 1994 he became the subject of endless sexual discourse that sought to make sense of him, this gaunt and striking figure who stood at odds with so much of what we expected a man in a rock band to be. There were no sharp edges or blunt corners to his form, every bit of the maze of questions found in his work. He wore a hat with the words "White House stop AIDS" in the midst of the ongoing AIDS crisis, and this, too, led people to ask questions as they did about any man who made public declarations of solidarity with those fighting a disease primarily afflicting LGBTQ+ people. There are always questions, and often they are not asked in good faith. Every time people wondered about Stipe, it made me wonder, and it made me lose myself in his work that much more. What secrets might be hidden there in his work?

"Man on the Moon" draws on the death of Kaufman as its central theme and with it looks at the world of possibility Kaufman chose to create around himself. That in all the darkness and unknowable dangers of a life, there is something magical to be found if we let ourselves look for it. Ask questions; there are always questions. Don't always accept the answer. Believe the lies that may help you make peace with what might otherwise be a life of endless torment.

In high school, one afternoon when the sun was too hot and the air was too dry, my friends and I craved respite from the brief months of endless sun in the Yukon summer. We drove up the road that trailed off through the cliffs behind my house, up another winding road darting around the cliffs and walking trails, then down to the clearings by the river where day camps and picnic tables were set up. I pulled my 1988 Datsun Maxima into a day camp site, opened the doors, and let punk rock mixtapes drown out bird songs and the sound of the river. We drank cheap beers and wine coolers stolen from older siblings' and parents' hiding places and found a world in which to survive.

The Yukon is often dark, often cold, isolated and removed from the world and plagued by the dangers lurking in banality. There's not often a whole lot to do other than develop habits that will come to haunt you in later years. But some days, like this one in the summertime, we could drive out to the water and pretend everything was always going to be just like this forever.

Andy Kaufman never wanted his story to be fully told. This is what we're led to believe as Jim Carrey method acts his way through his life in *Man on the Moon*, a movie titled after the R.E.M. song, which also appears on the film's soundtrack alongside "The Great Beyond," a song R.E.M. wrote for the film that attempts to honor a life of devilish half-truths and secrets to tell. Kaufman delighted in subverting truth and reality in life, subterfuge that followed him into death as rumors persist that he faked even that last and final act. Stipe sings about the impossible task of writing about a life that was never about the end, only ever about the thrill of the journey.

I'm pushing an elephant up the stairs.

At the pullout where we drank and drowned out our voices with punk rock records, there was a tire swing that swung out over the cold water of the Yukon River. This afternoon in the early summer, everyone took a turn swinging out over the water and jumping in. Everyone but me. Everyone but me and the anxious fears that plagued me. The endless tears and failure of my childhood that created this lifelong fear of going under the water. My friends were in the water, floating and laughing and chanting and calling for me to jump in. I couldn't tell them I was terrified of dying in the water like this.

R.E.M. worked on *Automatic for the People* in pieces. Peter Buck, Mike Mills, and Bill Berry created instrumental beds, and Michael Stipe came in after to populate the universe they had conjured with lives and love and loss and all the beautiful things that build the memory of a life. Lyrics were written in a panic as recording was winding down and Stipe just needed something, anything, that felt real. He couldn't arrive at the answer. Writer's block set in. The death of the artist. Days before the album needed to be finished, there were no words to fill in the blanks on what would be the second single from the album.

I took my glasses off out there in the campground by the river, my fear of water and death smothered just a little in stolen beer and skunk weed. Without glasses I am unable to see anything; the world becomes shapes and blotches, splatters of meaningless color. I heard the chants of my name and I couldn't respond with my fears. Instead, I walked out to the tire swing. Held onto the rope to test its strength. Took my clothes off and felt the naked body I hated feel the warmth of the sun.

I couldn't see it, or anything, and suddenly none of this mattered anymore. I couldn't see all the things I was afraid of, all the things I hated. I could see only shapes and possibilities.

Michael Stipe went on walks with headphones on and the bed tracks of what would become "Man on the Moon" playing in his ears. Looking for something, desperate for it to appear while he was roaming the streets of Seattle, where they were recording. Reflecting on the album for its twenty-fifth anniversary in 2017 with NPR's Robin Hilton, Stipe said of this song, "Andy Kaufman, somehow, became my Every Man. He became my Hero With a Thousand Faces. And these kinds of larger-than-life questions. Literally larger-than-life questions about existence and about what happens after we're gone, and did the man really walk on the moon?"

Standing naked out in a campsite by the Yukon River so close to my fears, I grabbed onto the rope and felt its weight and heard voices calling me in from the great beyond I couldn't see. The shapes and colors and blotches. I held on to the rope and felt my feet leave the ground and swung out past the ground and into the open air and felt freedom for a single second, and then immense and terrible panic as voices from below yelled in fear.

Stipe had been writing songs about death, because he was grappling with death at the time. His grandparents were aging, he had a dog falling deathly ill, he was dealing with the weight of the AIDS crisis. There was something in Kaufman that became the conduit through which Stipe wanted to process all of these things. These themes are present throughout *Automatic for the People*: death, loss, trauma, growing older, leaving youth behind. How to make sense of a life of sad and dark potholes on the road that led us here.

I couldn't see the ground or the water and didn't know when to let go. I could hear yelling but nothing clearly. I thought for sure I was going to die out there naked and half drunk and high on skunk weed in a campsite in the Yukon.

It was the Kaufman influence that helped Stipe find the words to "Man on the Moon." The references to Kaufman's life and career: Mister Fred Blassie and goofing on Elvis.

Hey baby.

It's Kaufman's spirit more than anything that became this conduit. How to find the strength to still ask questions in the face of stark and difficult truths. How to believe that not everything is as it seems to be. How to let go.

I thought I would die out there in the Yukon and decided to just let go and allow death to claim me. I didn't know if I was over the water or the land, but I just let go. Let go and dropped. My body in the air. I hated my body. Hated this life. Hated my fears. I fell in the air for seconds that felt like decades. I could hear voices yelling. I could hear the end rushing to me. And then my body hit the water with a loud splash and I sunk below the surface.

The story is that Stipe walked into the studio and laid down the vocals for "Man on the Moon" in a single take. They had taken so long to find him until suddenly they were there and ready and all he had to do was release them. Suddenly everything made sense and became clear. It is only in questioning everything, allowing yourself to believe that possibility exists in impossible places and that maybe not everything is as it appears, that it all becomes clear. Learning by failing, by not allowing the truth to interfere with our desire to make sense of the one life we are given. We can decide how our story will be told and how we might be remembered.

I was pulled up to the surface by hands and anxious shouts. I couldn't see, and I splashed about wildly as my body broke the tension of the surface. Panic. I must have looked like a feral animal dunked in a bathtub. Friends tried to calm me but couldn't. I hadn't told anyone of my fears. And now I couldn't even see to make sense of the world around me. I was floating in the water surrounded by shapes and colors and nothing and I wasn't dead. I was panicking; I was alive enough to panic. Hands held onto me with concern and fear until I finally found my center and could relax for a second. And then I laughed, laughed hard from somewhere in my body that had been holding on to so much fear for so long.

"Drive" is the thesis of *Automatic for the People*, laying out this theme of anxious growth into adulthood. It's haunting and dark and somber. It's the act of looking up the road and seeing death reflected in the taillights ahead. "Man on the Moon" is the answer to this fear, that death is only part of this story, not the end or the ultimate fear. That there is room here to question and wonder and allow ourselves to let go. To commit to the difficult bits and choose how we live this life. We don't know the truth of Kaufman's life, but we know how Michael Stipe imagines it as he sings to the end of it all. We don't know the secrets of death, and all we can do is find the right conduit to process our difficult feelings about the fear surrounding it. "Man on the Moon" sees the fear riding in "Drive" and begs you, you who are out swinging on a rope above what might be water or might be land, to just let go. Don't worry about the truth of all these difficult memories; you can still choose how you want to remember the hardest parts.

He might be a father but he sure ain't a dad

"ANDROGYNOUS"
THE REPLACEMENTS

Twice in my life I have learned the hard way to never trust a man who loves KISS. The first time was with a sexual predator masquerading as a baker in the grocery store when I was too young to know better, and the second was in Alberta in the early 2000s.

When I agreed to train to take over my dad's position as manager at our glass shop back home in Whitehorse—a shop that was part of a chain of western Canadian glass shops—I had to first prove myself worthy of the position by working at an All West Glass outpost in Edmonton.

By now I had worked in a variety of glass shops, and the experience was always the same, entering into rooms with scores of men obsessed with the merits of their own masculinity and putting it on display for you and all to see. Not to exert dominance or establish order, but to let you know who they intend to be in relation to you. Guards up, everyone. I walked into the break room in the All West Glass shop in Edmonton, which was the same kind of break room you found in every building in every profession where the idea of a break is often treated as a farcical novelty. A white table stained with the detritus of food that had lived and died on its surface, a microwave that had killed more meals than it cooked, and the faint smell of shitty coffee leaking out from a steel urn on a counter, next to a sink no one dared use. It was wretched and perfect.

The staff, my future coworkers, went about releasing their names and information to me. The salesman who claimed to be a member of Mensa and prided himself on being the smartest redneck in the woods. The jaded journeyman who spent most days on jobsites smoking cigarettes in a truck with the windows rolled up, peppering his lungs to obtain the right grit to yell at anyone who dared cross him. The shop foreman who was more amiable than most, the only one to introduce himself with a light-hearted joke, a laugh, and a smile. A man who you knew had seen troubles and chose to move through them by finding the light left in the world around him. The mysterious stranger lying about his history, a man who claimed a lot of backstory that remained unverifiable and always seemed a little false. He had a dog named Bones that rode with him in his truck who was missing a bit of his tongue, sliced off by an errant piece of glass. The worst turn in the introduction field was the self-obsessed man who envisioned himself as a gift from God to the others around him, running his hand through a head of auburn hair while he bragged about himself for longer than anyone asked for.

The first day I met this room of people, they asked me an urgent question, a detail they needed well before my name or background or work history. They asked if I was one of them. They didn't clarify what they meant by the statement, but I could feel the intention behind each syllable. They couldn't even say the word. They couldn't bring themselves to ask, "Are you gay?," not because they knew it was wrong but because they couldn't acknowledge the weight of the word they felt in their hearts.

I sat down at a white bench seat among them, poured a cup of shitty coffee, and said quietly and carefully, "I don't know what you mean." Fear and bitterness formed in my throat as I spoke. I wanted them to say it, these men so proud and strong; I wanted them to ask me directly.

The man with perfect hair told me plainly that the last man who had worked here, the one whose position I was filling, had been a poofter. These grown men couldn't say *gay* but felt that calling someone a poofter was a fitting substitute.

I have moved from city to city, job to job, and in each place felt my gender and sexuality questioned and challenged. I knew what I was hiding, and so I naturally obsessed about how it was showing on my face. I denied my status as a poofter, though truth be told, the more men in my industry challenged me on my performance of masculinity, the more pride in myself I felt.

I used to think that I stood wrong.

When you're standing at the bank counter, waiting for the teller to type for an awfully long time while you deposit a check that's lighter than you'd like it to be, have you ever considered how you stand in that moment? I was obsessed with it. I didn't stand straight and tall; I had not so much as a casual lean. I felt awkward, like Bambi finding her legs for the first time. Sometimes I shifted, my legs swaying from side to side, or I held a leg slightly up like a flamingo haunting a perfect lawn on the sun-soaked streets of an idyllic suburban landscape. I always thought that I was failing spectacularly, like there was some perfect way to stand that let the men around you know that you knew the rules. Sometimes I thought there was a handbook everyone else got that I missed out on.

I was a punk rock kid from a young age because in punk rock I felt the most safe in my desire to be something else, something different and a little queer. Punk rock was sold to me, to all of us, as a place to be different, and it wasn't until later that I saw that it was often a place to be different as long as you were committed to being the same.

A punk rock kid in redneck country who was worried about how I stood at the bank counter while men I didn't know asked whether I was one of them. The dreaded other. Always looking for a place to stand.

I always thought about the time I got the shit beat out of me by the man who felt that I was a little too gregarious for his liking. Men liked to beat the idea into me that I wasn't like them in an effort to harden me somehow, hammer a keen edge onto my blunt and dull surface. After hitting me enough times, he tried to reframe the whole ordeal as a step in his own sinister lesson plan on budding masculinity, told me this was all for my own good. You'll see, he said.

In the wake of the violence, he asked me what music I liked—an abuser builds a bridge—and I said I liked punk rock as it always made me feel tough despite my slight frame and awkward nature. There in the aftermath of violence, I told him about the bands that I liked, the palm mutes and power chords of southern Californian skate punk bands, and he laughed and told me those bands wouldn't make me grow up in any proper way. I had to learn to be a man. That's why he hit me, you know. He told me to listen to Black Flag, and he told me about the Replacements.

There's something about the idea of hiding brilliance under a layer of half-truths and subterfuge that is part of the charm of the Replacements. A band of people that are easily read as misfits, these ramshackle alley cats masquerading as men. The original lineup of singer/guitarist Paul Westerberg, drummer Chris Mars, child prodigy Tommy Stinson on bass, and his brother Bob on guitar, until he was kicked out of the band and replaced by Slim Dunlap and then Steve Foley.

Initially calling themselves Dogbreath, the Replacements can be traced back to the classic strain of vintage dad rock that left a generation's garages and seeped into punk rock basements soaked in cheap beer and lost drugs. Here was a band of men—initially Bob, Tommy, and Chris—trying to find themselves. Bob was eight years older than his younger brother Tommy, a high school dropout who was given a bass to provide some kind of structure. Something for his hands to do that might not cause as much trouble as a listless life on the streets of their home in Minneapolis. Westerberg joined the band when he heard the music they were conjuring emerging from an open window as he walked home from his janitorial job.

The Replacements are the kind of band you build legends around, self-destructive young men so afraid of their own talents they chose instead to blow them up at every opportunity. They chose the name the Replacements as a self-deprecating cut to their own skin. As Chris Mars once said, "Like maybe the main act doesn't show, and instead the crowd has to settle for an earful of us dirtbags. . . . It seemed to sit just right with us, accurately describing our collective 'secondary' social esteem."

The first time I heard about the Replacements, they were not described in loving detail. This was typical, as a generation of angry men looking to justify their own misplaced anger and ire read only the surface of the band, the drinking and the drugs, and the explosion. See only the fire; never mind the tinder and oxygen required to build a flame. I told myself that day, with the bruises forming in hidden places on my body, I would never like this band. Who could love men who reveled in this kind of abject violence, who hated themselves so much?

It would take years until I learned to love how I hated myself too.

I hated myself for not telling these men in this break room that I was a fucking poofter, whatever the fuck that means. The word made me angry, its bitter hatred that sprang forth from grown men using childish words to describe the real life of people they despised. The man who fancied himself a philosopher in khaki and camouflage who took every chance he could to turn a two-dollar word into a ten-dollar exchange but couldn't find it in himself to use the word *gay* or even any of the better slurs. But I said nothing. I stayed silent, which was only worse. In silence, answers become facts without words or confirmation, and so I swiftly and cowardly protested any hint of poofterism in my system.

Everyone in the shop knew that I was there to learn how to replace my dad at our shop back home, our small store nestled away in the Yukon, in contrast to the size and inflated importance of the million-people-strong city I found myself in now.

The sign upon driving into the city proudly proclaimed this to be the city of champions because Wayne Gretzky had led the Edmonton Oilers to Stanley Cup victories, and this is the sort of thing you let define you if you never once cared about anything real.

In a kind of working-class nepotism, I had been brought into the industry by my dad and given opportunities to advance within it with his guidance. There is a privilege in this, as there is in all things. Manual labor is an often cruel and difficult field, where simply working hard is not always guaranteed to offer you a better station in life. We are sold this lie in our youth. That with hard work comes great reward, when more often it is people who are lucky, the ones who know the right person or have the right last name, who are given opportunities not afforded to all. It is also true that the privilege of being able to become the owner of a local outpost of a western chain of glass shops is different than your dad getting you into an Ivy League school or a cushy job at a tower of window and wealth downtown. But it is privilege all the same, and people could see that on me too. The mark of a guarantee in life and the concern that I wasn't good enough to deserve its being pinned to me.

My only savior was the ability and desire to see myself destroyed. I've had intrusive thoughts for as long as I remember. Stray words in my head. The most prominent are always urges to destroy. After the first time I was in a car wreck as a teenager—when a coworker and I rear-ended a Toyota on an icy road on our way home from work—I wanted one to truly mangle me, to need to be rebuilt. To destroy all that I was, dismantle all the bones and muscle of me enough that I could be regathered as someone new, someone real, someone ideal and perfect. Someone who stood the right way at the bank and had the right kind of body and was never suspected of being wrong. This is how all the worst urges appear, as flotsam in the wreckage of my mind when my guard is down. They pass through, nest inside my worst fears, and build a life for themselves. I didn't want to be the perception of me, but I thought the only way to find myself was in immolation.

I wonder this about the Replacements. Though I promised myself I would never love this band, it was impossible to avoid because I had the same crush on Jennifer Love Hewitt that everyone else had in the late 1990s, and in 1998 I saw the movie *Can't Hardly Wait*.

The right soundtrack at the right time can break the world in front of you, and while *Can't Hardly Wait* is a movie whose plot did not remain in my memory, the soundtrack lived in my car and in my head for decades to come. It was an early proponent of "Dammit" as Blink-182 was only beginning to emerge as the band that would change the face of punk rock as power pop. It propelled a summer of perfect house parties soundtracked by the Busta Rhymes single "Turn It Up (Remix)/Fire It Up" (a remix of "Turn It Up" from *When Disaster Strikes*, now featuring a sample of the theme song to *Knight Rider*) and the song playing over the credits, the Replacements' "Can't Hardly Wait."

In my misled youth I had mistakenly believed that the Replacements were a band of excessive waste and abject destruction. But here there was truth; playing over the credits of an upper-mid-tier late '90s high school party movie was a bright and playful guitar, chords repeating and drawing you in before Westerberg's voice towered over all things, tender but scratched, cracked and lived in. The promise of something real, never perfect. I watched the credits scroll all the way through, seconds felt like hours until they ran through the soundtrack, and there at the bottom was "Can't Hardly Wait," the Replacements, and all the things I had believed to be true were a lie all at once.

Just as I was raised by my life at home, with the influence of my mom and dad and an older sister, I was raised by record stores and the life within them. Life lessons drawn from racks of CDs and burnout employees who held eager knowledge of the world to be found in the breadth of their empire. I never held much weight in scholastic studies but trusted that all I ever needed to know I could learn from the right CD at the right moment. While this had not proven to be particularly useful for graduation purposes, it has carried me through decades of life all the same.

I asked at the record store about the Replacements, and in the used bin there was a copy of *Let It Be* with an image of four tired and bleary-eyed men of indeterminate age sitting on a rooftop washed out in blue light for four dollars, and I was told this was the best place to start. Record store bargain bins are where all perfect journeys begin. I knew *Can't Hardly Wait* and was prepared for more of the same, an education in all that they had built, and was unprepared for how hard I would be hit by the opening shambolic dust cloud of "I Will Dare."

In 1998 when I played *Let It Be* for the first time, I was sixteen years old and fashioned myself a punk rocker but only by way of what was emerging as the dominate subculture of Fat Wreck Chords and its adjacent homogeneity. Hearing the Replacements be described as a punk rock band caused me to have to reconsider the mental math of all that I had known to be true. If this was punk rock, then what had I been other than a lie? There was no shade of endlessly repeated power chords and pogo jumps here; Westerberg and crew seemed to be at once obsessed with the classic rock associated with stations that had once played on radios overlooking vintage cars in some sepia-toned garages somewhere and also running through the work of the Stooges and a pile of discarded cigarettes. They were rough and dirty and raw and angry, but angry with purpose. They were fighting against something, even and often when it was just themselves. Fighting to find something better in their lives to live for.

I pushed myself as hard as I could in the glass shop. I lifted more than I was able, wrapped tape and paper towels on my wounds that emerged from knives and glass on my skin, and kept going through the pain that coursed through the bone and sinew of my slender frame that had never planned to shore up its defenses for what I was putting it through. Blood on my body and tired muscles were just signs of my strength, a mark of how much I earned the opportunity ahead of me. Every time someone questioned how much I deserved the opportunity I had, I would throw myself that much harder at the job in hopes that in pain and blood and suffering I could be seen.

Every lunch and every break the men gathered in our shitty break room and proceeded to brag and boast about all the things that will never become important, making casual references to how they wish the poofter that left had stuck around long enough to be killed by them. There is no hyperbole when I tell you that every crew at every job I have ever worked have talked openly to me about their desire and ability to kill any perceived queerness in the world, and each time they spoke of their thirst for blood I bristled. I had longer hair when I started working there, and I swiftly shaved it down to a tight buzz. Carried myself taller than I was, harder than I was. Lowered my voice another register when I could. Smoked and drank and hurt and hid myself away in favor of feeling safe around the bloodthirsty bigots I had to suffer. Men I can so clearly see, now that they are in the rearview, were sad and broken but at the time were just terrifying towers that served as a warning of all worst cases come to life.

The beauty of the Replacements, and there is much to be found, is in the cracks in all of their foundations. They are legendary as men born of self-immolation that ruined any and all possibility of a fruitful career. Getting so drunk at shows they would forget their own songs, sometimes playing while wearing dresses or becoming hostile with what audience they could find. The band most people think of when trivia gets raised about the people who are no longer welcome back to 30 Rock to appear on *Saturday Night Live* after a spectacular master class of mayhem wherein Bob Stinson infamously had to borrow a guitar from G. E. Smith and the SNL band because he got so fucked up before they went on that he tripped in the hall en route to the stage for their second performance and broke his own guitar.

But in all the flames of a life they put on display, the true beauty of the Replacements was all the things they hid in the fire. Westerberg more than most is a poet of the world he sees in front of him, a bard of all the perfect things we find in tired lives lived on worn-out streets. Westerberg and the Replacements are champions for generations of young people who feel they don't deserve enough, don't come from the right houses or feel lifted by the right wealth. The Mats, a nickname for the band that is a truncated take on the Placemats, instead urge the realization that none of these things matter, not our names or places but our hearts and lives. We will all grow with scars and bruises, but those are only there to prove that we lived as hard as we could.

It beats picking cotton, and waiting to be forgotten.

There is a weekend that resides forever in my memories. The good hair man and I had to go out of town for a job. We would be gone three days, working together, sharing a hotel, and eating together, and I dreaded every moment of it. On our way out of the city, facing six hours of travel time in a truck not big enough for all the ego and animosity we brought as baggage, he talked at length and told the same tired stories he had told again and again at the break room table about the conquests of his life. He had once been the owner of a massive shop—the biggest and best in the city—an empire of glass built by him and his business partners, and for a while they lived as large as possible. With his hands on the wheel of a truck speeding nowhere, he told me about the endless parties, the blow and the booze and the nights they spent at strip clubs, where he had fashioned himself into a lothario of legend, this man loved by all who loved in return bragging about the women he slept with and his masculinity that bordered always on obscenely comical. He told me about how when the internet came online and he started to corral women he called his "internet whores," it took a year for his wife to find out. How she had unfairly thrown him out of the house. How his business partners had given him an ultimatum about his drinking and his cocaine and how unfair it was that they removed him from the company even after he promised to get sober. And he did; after his wife kicked him out and women on the internet stopped allowing him to emotionally manipulate them and his company continued on without him, he got sober.

We drove and he asked me what kind of music I liked. Everything always felt like a test with these men, there was always a right answer, and I said the Replacements and he said he had never heard of them. So I played "I Will Dare" for a minute before he told me to "turn this fag shit off," and with each of the three letters of that word his fangs showed themselves and I remembered I was not always safe. He asked me about my love life, was I dating anyone, and very carefully forced my hand to announce the gender of my partners. I had been dating a woman at the time, and he seemed relieved at my perceived heterosexuality. He commandeered the aux cable and played "Love Gun" by KISS, told me if I wanted to be a real man and learn how to please a woman this is what I needed to listen to. He told me about his obsession with Gene Simmons. I had been here before with a predatory man, and every praise of the work of this band was another red flag in a crimson field.

That weekend we had to share a hotel and also a room, and I was told in very plain language that he had to do this once before with the poofter and he would tell me the same thing he told him, that if it looked like I started to get curious he would kill me in my sleep. And then the first evening after we were done working, he disappeared. For hours and hours I had no idea where he was, we had no cell signal and no means of communicating, and he was just gone somewhere. As I lay in bed half asleep, he barged into the room carried by the stench of falling off the wagon and proceeded to do blow with a sex worker on his bed and yelled loudly about how I should wake up and see how a man, a real man, operates. I pretended to be asleep, or maybe dead, and wished I could be. And then in the morning he was gone.

The rest of the weekend I worked alone. He never appeared back at our hotel even once. I looked for him on streets and in alleys, asked the front desk and made calls that provided no answers, so all I could do was pack his bags and load them in the truck when it was time to leave. I knew he would find his own way or die out there, and I found myself not caring either way. I was relieved that the drive back belonged just to me and not to the misplaced ego of a man who cared only about desperately clinging to glories he had never earned.

He might be a father but he sure ain't a dad.

I played "Androgynous" out on the road alone, a stark contrast to the excess and clownish makeup of KISS. "Androgynous" is the Replacements well ahead of their time. A piano ballad hidden in a circle pit, a hopeful celebration of love and desire that might transcend gender and identity. Dick is wearing a skirt; Jane is wearing a chain. They are androgynous and free, and there is no malice or spite in his voice.

In all the posturing and chest thumping of men around me in the world, I rarely felt they were real. Peacocks throwing their feathers for all to see, in desperate hope that someone might notice their own self-perceived splendor. The Replacements instead lived a life enraptured with possibility that all things might be true, that anything is possible, and that there is nothing we cannot dream of, and this is no more or better made true than in "Androgynous." The band sees the difference and queerness of the world and never finds reasons to mock and terrify it, but rather sees it as portent of possibility, that if we were to let our guards and our prejudices down and open ourselves up to something beautiful then we could change the way we seek and find love. Change the way we dress and the way we are free. North America loves to pride itself on some self-described freedom, but at so many turns are we given outlines to stay within.

The Replacements, these four men in blue on a rooftop, offered a way out by refusing to be constrained by the boundaries of tradition or the sneers of those who position themselves as better. By choosing to be more than the scars of their past and marking a new path, loud and brash, chasing love and destruction all at once. By destroying the barriers of the old world and living reckless and free.

Last night I dreamt I'd forgotten my name

"I WISH I WAS THE MOON"

NEKO CASE

My name, the one given to me by my parents when I was born, was an accident. Initially, they were going to name me Spencer, a decision they thankfully forgot on the way to the hospital to bring me into the world. They named me   and gave me the middle name Stanley, after my grandfather. As they were writing it down, they realized at the last minute that my initials would spell ASS, and that felt like setting me up for failure. So they pivoted and gave me two middle names: Gerald and George, after two men I never met. I never liked my name, and I never fully understood why.

I have never believed in God, but I have always asked him for favors. When I was a kid and my bedroom was on the second floor of our house, with my window facing out into the night, I lay awake in the captain's bed I slept in and stared into the sky, imagining God listening and cataloging the desires of all the people trapped here in the place he left for us. I asked to be remade, to wake up new. Not as a prayer, rather I begged and pleaded and made promises. Maybe this is just what praying feels like to firm believers.

I have begged that God might change me, but I have never believed God was real, and we cannot rely on the things we don't believe in to ever save us. We can only trust the strength of what desires we can hold in our own hands.

I have worked with my hands my entire life. These hands stocked the grocery store shelves. These hands worked fashion retail and sold Cuban cigars to American tourists. These hands worked for years with my dad at All West Glass, the glass shop he ran down on Fourth Avenue. I started working for him when I was young, grew old and tired and angry in the walls of that shop, gained experience under the sound of power tools, men's voices, and the distant static of the radio.

The first time I heard Neko Case was on that radio, over the din of men working and yelling and sweating and bleeding. Midafternoon in the fall on a nameless day in the Yukon of my youth, the dirt on the floor mixed with a green powder we sprinkled on it to minimize dirt that smelled a bit like old coffee and new mold. CBC Radio played in the background, the faint sound of public broadcasting the counterweight to whatever intensity lingered in the air as we pushed ourselves to keep going. Hard and tired bodies, always moving. If there is time to lean, there is time to clean. There is only time to push on. Bleed and move and sweat, and only stop when there is nothing left to fight for.

I was replacing a shattered windshield in a 1988 GMC Suburban, my arms reaching over a weathered dashboard to cut away at the urethane bonding the broken glass to a crumbling metal frame succumbing to rust and time. A tree had fallen and crushed this windshield in the middle, and the only way to cut it away was to use my left arm to hold the broken glass in place so it didn't fall on my neck and shoulders and use my free arm to slice away at the glue. Get it loose enough that I could lean back in a well-worn driver's seat and kick it out with my steel-toe boots. Worry about the bleeding later, worry about the way your back hurts in the lower and the left sides because of the way you have to twist your wiry frame around to slice and kick and push and bleed all at once.

In the midst of all this, a Neko Case song came on in between interviews with local mining experts and city councilors pushing for reelection despite never once living up to the faint promises of their office. Case's voice caught me, there behind the dash of a Suburban with a shard of glass stuck in my arm. I knew it was bleeding but I couldn't really move, and blood was just something I had learned to accept. I came to welcome it as a sign that I had pushed myself as hard as possible. Put some paper towel and tape on the spot where blood was emerging and kept going.

I was not paying attention to the music until I couldn't help it, until Case's voice wrapped around me with smoky weight that announces itself like an army at the gates. It was an instant and easy obsession with the tones and timbers of her voice, dipping low like a bird gliding above the surface of a lake, only to shoot for the heavens to accent the potential of its otherworldly beauty. I didn't know who she was, but I listened for words so I could have phrases to remember her by.

I'm so lonely.

My body shivered at each syllable, the word *lonely* stretched to its breaking point, and I promised myself I would learn all I could about the woman attached to this voice. A radio host mentioned a name: Neko Case. I didn't hear the song title but remembered enough of the words to write them on my arm in permanent marker. Below where a piece of paper towel was taped to my arm and the dried blood staining it, I scrawled "Niko (?) Case, last night I dreamt I'd forgotten my name."

I walked home from work that day, my body aching with each step on the crumbling pavement that eventually turned into a dirt road, up Alexander Street to Eighth Avenue, where I lived in a basement apartment that sounded haunted every time the heat came on. The pipes that ran through the ceiling were too big for the holes drilled to hold them, and every time they heated up and expanded they banged against their surroundings and made a loud clang and popping sound. The decibels of hitting your limitations in this world.

I got home, typed the words fading on my arm into my computer, and waited to see what came of it. I searched Niko Case, found that I had spelled her name wrong. Neko. A member of the New Pornographers, an indie-rock/power-pop supergroup who were already big on music blogs in the early 2000s with their album *Twin Cinema* and the video for "Lose It" featuring the stars of LA's exploding alt-comedy scene. On forums people talk about the New Pornographers being Canadian, which feels both exotic and benign from within.

I looked for what information I could find on Neko Case. She isn't technically Canadian. She was born in Virginia, moved from city to city before letting her roots grow deeper in Tacoma, Washington, until she moved to Vancouver,

British Columbia, in the '90s to attend the Emily Carr Institute of Art and Design. Spend enough time in Vancouver and you are, at the very least, step-Canadian. She played in legendary Vancouver bands Cub and Maow, two of many that emerged in Vancouver's nascent punk rock scene in the early to mid-'90s. She was an artist, a drummer. She didn't sing in front of anyone until she was in her twenties.

Neko Case is an artist written in legends. This woman with fiery red hair and a voice that could shatter glass just as easily as it could form it from sand and nothing. She appears almost otherworldly, possessed of a spirit that fears no limitations. The juxtaposition between the power-pop and balladry of the New Pornographers and the world drawn in her solo work that trades in country and roots origins. Her work is the promise of moving between worlds and finding yourself thriving in all places.

The year before I discovered Neko Case, I had been living in Alberta with my girlfriend. We did not have a good or healthy relationship, largely because I was too afraid of myself to let my guard down, but I am nothing if not obsessed with holding on to all things and people like an emotional hoarder, and I tried too hard to make it work without owning the fact that I was the problem. I believed so hard I could force it to work, like you could force yourself to believe in God. Like I could make the lie become real if I thought long and hard about the possibilities of its truths.

She was the first person I ever came out as trans to, in Red Deer, Alberta, while "How You Remind Me" by Nickelback played in the background at the onset of its popularity, and you cannot imagine a worse place to come out as trans for the very first time in 2001. She didn't take it very well, but I didn't handle any of this with grace either, and it dissolved what was left between us. We broke up and she moved on, started a family and a career and grew up. I became insular and angry at myself, taking it out on the life around me instead of doing the work I needed on my head and my heart.

I moved around a bit after that, moved to Calgary and then Edmonton and back between all of these places. Nothing ever seemed to work or fit, and if God was ever real He surely would have carefully guided me away from this province in the midst of an oil boom proving toxic to my heart.

In my youth, into young and then older adulthood, I was quick to quit. Life often asked hard questions, and it was easier to drop everything and flee instead of listening to the desires burning where I stood. Leave behind all of my shortcomings and setbacks. A life of failures, living like a fire running wild through dry underbrush.

I always ended up back home, back in the Yukon, because it was where I felt the safest, but this was only ever partly true. Safety by way of the familiarity of a small town. Streets teeming with faces without names that all know each other and their business. Outside the safety of this I could be anyone, and there is nothing more terrifying than possibility if you are already scared of your own truth. Better to hide it, better to blend in, better to be safe. A face with a name that feels familiar.

"I WISH I WAS THE MOON" is one of many standout tracks on Neko Case's third record, 2002's *Blacklisted*. There's a legend in here, too, that she was blacklisted from the Grand Ole Opry for taking her shirt off at an outdoor Opry performance. The truth is something different, that she likely had heat stroke and wasn't making some grand fuck-you statement to the long-running Americana institution, but the truth is never as good a story as a legend and a catchy name.

Case hadn't started as a country musician; she started in punk rock and art scenes, moved cities and genres. Leaned into power pop with the New Pornographers, recorded vocals for their debut record *Mass Romantic* as she was leaving Canada for Seattle with the loss of her student visa. Even with the New Pornographers, sharing vocal duties with Carl Newman and Dan Bejar (Destroyer), her voice takes up like a storm and shakes the shutters loose, demanding attention. Her voice is the product of a life of curious discovery, the voice of rifling through a record store and finding Bowie and Wanda Jackson and ELO and Thin Lizzy all at once. An artistic journey through influences that build to a single point. Case's voice has always been the point of entry to her music, or at least it was for me, and it's only in crossing the threshold into the world of her songwriting that you can be so ecstatically lost in her haunting and beautiful phrases.

It is hard to hate the entry point to your own life, but I hated my name. When I was in high school and I started to make friends, people abandoned my first name. They called me Stratis, like a rogue cop or a model prisoner. My first name held no power or meaning to me; every time it was used I thought someone was talking about a different person. This disembodied name attached to a face that was never there. When people asked what it was, I mumbled through it, and it became an amalgamation of consonants and vowels that always proved interesting when it was spelled on to-go cups in busy coffee shops. I joked that I said my own name wrong as I rushed through it. Partners and lovers would tell me it was

weird to call me Stratis and also weird to call me ,
and both were true.

Neko Case did not have a good relationship with her parents. It is not for me to speculate and I can only go off interviews and snippets, but she has spoken on the nature of the relationship between them, telling the *New York Times* in 2009, "I've been mourning my dad my whole life," and NPR in 2013, "They've never really been my parents. . . . They are my biological parents but they never wanted a kid and so I just wasn't really parented."

"I Wish I Was the Moon" is easily read as the fallout of a relationship that no longer served the heart of its narrator.

God blessed me, I'm a free man, with no place free to go.

An easy read of songs about relationships is that they are always romantic, but there is too much faith in never questioning or considering all the relationships that build a life, the ones that bind us by the names we trade with each other. What if she was singing to the troubled distance put between herself and her parents?

Last night I dreamt I'd forgotten my name
'Cause I sold my soul
But I woke just the same.

When pleading to God doesn't work, eventually you might consider what the devil may offer. God never once responded to my pleas and prayers, and while I never made inroads on conjuring the devil, I made it known I was willing to parlay. Anything to change my body, my life, my name.

I've always been lucky to have a good relationship with my parents, despite it not always being an easy road for us. Being a parent is a hard and often thankless task, and not everyone is up for it; not everyone is good at it or desires it. Parents and their children have complicated connections, and sometimes severing toxic tethers is the best you can do. There are plenty of mothers and fathers in this world, but fewer moms and dads. A mother and father bring life into the world; moms and dads do their level best to raise them, show them the way, impart what lessons they know.

Deals with God and the devil never worked out, and as I grew older, into my twenties and then my thirties, I started to ground my plans in reality. How to separate myself from my name. This burning desire to be who I knew I was and had buried deep inside all the locked corners of my body was never going away, and in desperation I made plans. Plans to fake my own death, plans to secede from family and home. I thought I would be so unloved and unlovable in the life I desired for myself, transness burning holes in my soul desperate to be real. I had tried to come out and it had never worked, and it felt like I knew I was making a bad decision. Maybe all I had left were bad decisions.

I thought the only way to be alive was to just one day disappear. I wanted that to be the job of gods and devils because I wanted there to be some trick of divine intervention that let everyone forget that   had ever been real at all. Let me be erased and reborn; I was willing to be alone when I did. These were the terms I offered to deities I didn't believe in but would accept help from all the same.

It's harder to make the decisions yourself to take what you need from this life and know that you might lose people along the way. It's harder to accept the responsibility of distance from names and faces and hearts you have known for days and weeks and years. To be trans is to be someone new, and familiar faces don't always like new in place of the old.

Neko Case moved her roots in the years after leaving her step-Canadian home in Vancouver. She left for Seattle, released her debut solo album, *The Virginian*, credited to Neko Case & Her Boyfriends, in 1997 and began laying the bricks that would become a path to follow. Where she had been playing in punk bands in Canada, now she was leaning into her country and Americana roots, learning to trust her voice and her desires. In 2000 she released the follow-up *Furnace Room Lullaby*, finding a comfortable stability in the strength of her voice and now exploring darker depths in her songwriting. The title track, recorded with Travis Good of legendary Canadian band the Sadies, is a murder ballad complete with telltale heart motifs and a body buried deep under the floorboards of the living.

The murder ballad is traditionally a song crafted in a man's narrative, often writing about the death of a woman in their orbit, a cheating wife or a scorned lover. Case joins the ranks of the bold women—artists like Dolly Parton, Wanda Jackson, the Chicks, and more—in country and Americana reclaiming their personhood in a genre seeking to write them only as objects, as victims.

There is something beautiful found in embracing the darkness. Around the release of *Furnace Room Lullaby*, Case left Seattle for Chicago, where she would release *Blacklisted*, removing the boyfriends from her name and allowing herself to stand alone on the stage. *Blacklisted* further cemented her place as a songwriter deftly capable of wading into dark water to dredge out songs of tremendous and terrifying beauty. Dramatic and atmospheric, she wields her voice like a swinging ax stalking you from around dark corners, taunting you deeper into the abyss. She credited the work of David Lynch and his frequent collaborator, the composer Angelo Badalamenti, as inspirations in her work. How to craft a darkness you can't help but find yourself drawn to, how to crave the embrace of all our darkest impulses.

Case creates a world in which loss and pain and darkness can add as many stones as they want to the well of the heart; there is no less opportunity to keep going, to embrace with tender care the hard and difficult places we find ourselves and learn to keep going. Accept the responsibility of the hard decisions we make. Case moved from city to city seeking to make a life, made distance from relationships that didn't work and held on to those that did. Made a life in her name.

I could never fake my death because I could not bring myself to sever my life from my name, no matter how much it didn't serve me. When I did eventually come out, I planned to lose it all. I came out to friends slowly and carefully until finally I knew I had to tell my family. I told my mom my hard and difficult truth on my way to drop her off to a doctor's appointment. She offered to tell my dad for me, and in the intervening minutes between these tells I called my sister, who said, "I have to run to a meeting, and you choose now to tell me I could have always had a sister?" My mom told my dad, who in turn told me he was mad. Mad that I thought he would be upset, that this would distance us from each other. And that he only wants me to be safe, to be happy.

They asked about my name. Everyone wanted to know about my name when I came out. There are some who had no idea I ever had a first name because calling me by my last name—my family name—had become ubiquitous. I was scared for the first time to lose it.

When I first came out I struggled to land on a name, initially choosing a new one that didn't work for me. I was trying to please other people in building a new life and clumsily made a new name that incorporated parts of the old. It worked only as piece of worn tape holding old lives and new ones together. When it all started to fall apart and I knew I needed to find my own, I thought long and hard about the women who helped build me here. In a friend's living room in Toronto, there was a picture of Nico walking through Times Square in an elegant suit, and I thought about her as this vision for who I wanted to be. The first time I tried on the name it felt perfect, like finding an old shirt that fits you just right in all the places you desire to be held by familiar cloth. I thought about Neko Case, too, thought about how I would rather not spell my name with a "c" and tie my namesake to the life of a timeless singer who was nonetheless an avowed racist. I thought about not wanting to steal someone's life in order to build my own name.

When I needed to find who I was, I wrote down a name that I had misspelled on my arm in permanent marker many years earlier, below blood and glass, and returned to a life I had dreamed of, begged gods and devils for. A name that came to me hearing "I Wish I Was the Moon" playing through blown-out speakers on the CBC Radio of a life left in the darkness behind me. I went back to find the clues left behind and found Niko.

Take my hand and help me not to shake

"YOU'RE ALRIGHT"

SHARON VAN ETTEN

I'm an addict. I know this. I know this because whenever I become obsessed with something and can't let it go, I will so easily tell myself it's not a problem. It's not affecting me. Not just substances, not just booze or drugs or cigarettes, but ideas. I am haunted by the whispery spectral presence of ideas. I can and will spend a lifetime obsessing about their intricate possibilities.

I have a stack of magazines I have kept over the years, through apartments and personal downsizing of trash to thrift. Among them: copies of *The Believer*, a magazine about the Beastie Boys released after MCA passed away, and a series of lit mags called *The Great Discontent* that features interviews with artists that cross all creative boundaries. Photographers, comedians, writers, musicians. It is a large-format print magazine with beautiful photos and lengthy interviews, printed on that perfect kind of paper, smooth with a hint of texture like well-worn sandpaper.

Each issue is themed: the "Leaps" issue with Tavi Gevinson on the cover, the "Possibility" issue with Alison Sudol, the "Ambition" issue with Leon Bridges, and the one that lived on my desk for many years, dog-eared and bookmarked—the "Hustle" issue with Sharon Van Etten.

Interviewed in 2014 after the release of her fourth record, *Are We There*, Van Etten is charming, open, and forthcoming about the hustle and the road she had traveled to her current place. In 2012 she had released *Tramp*, working with the National's Aaron Dessner as a producer long before he became the go-to for Taylor Swift and others, looking to bring a backwoods charm to pop idealism.

With *Tramp*, Van Etten shifted from indie-folk darling to an emergent voice of great beauty and tremendous potential. The indie landscape in the mid-2010s was starting to shift and reform, and it brought new footing for folk and adjacent genres to have a place to stand. By no means a perfect experiment, the broadsheet of a browser scrolling through the likes of *Pitchfork* found a break in a fanatical adherence to covering men to bring in the occasional woman and congratulate itself with little self-reflection about the glaring lack of intersectional change at the altar of middle American white people.

Tramp was released in February 2012, four months before I was to turn thirty. I was living in an apartment above a garage on Eighth Avenue in downtown Whitehorse, the avenue that pavement forgot, a dirt road that turned to oceans of potholes in the rain. Behind us was a cliff, and the stairs that traveled up it for people who chose to walk to the airport or foolish runners who wanted to kill themselves in training by running up and down them.

We lived down here, my then-partner Alison and I, in a small apartment built by a five-foot-tall man and designed for his reach, in stark contrast to my six-foot-two frame. We opened the bedroom door, put our queen-size bed in the tiny room, and decided that for the rest of our tenure in this space the door would never close again. We had moved there in 2011, just as Alison was prepping to return to school in Vancouver, and I remained behind to capture the feeling of this small place alone. Alone except for her cat, a grey tabby named Charlie, whose moving in I had protested, saying I'm not even a cat person, until the minute his paws crossed our threshold and he set about deciding I was his favorite. Charlie's arrival made me question every truth I had held so close and dear.

Our little above-garage closet masquerading as an apartment was an endless exercise in abject frustrations. A narrow hallway that claimed status as a kitchen. The little living room with a big, beautiful window and magnificent view of downtown Whitehorse, facing the apartment I had been living in the basement of when Alison and I first met, on a night when a cadre of doomed romantics and ongoing alcoholics had drunk ourselves into our stools at a bar a friend owned at the tail end of Main Street, a bar that used to be the sort of Yukon scene that had blood soaked into the carpet from the endless fights of previous evenings and a filthy bathroom, save all the tops of toilet tanks where people did cocaine to stay up for all the dark nights of the endless winter.

Now this bar was clean and gentrified, and we spent hours there drinking with staff discounts even though we didn't work there, gambling by playing a game we simply called the Game that no one can remember the rules to anymore. The night I met Alison I won $100 playing the Game then threw up in a urinal, and somehow we fell in love all the same.

We fell in love despite the fact that I rejected her after we spent the night together. The day after we first met, I was still a little drunk and impulsively jumped on a plane to Vancouver, met a former model from Macedonia who sparked a swift and doomed romance that involved her attempting to recruit me for a work farm she was building in northern British Columbia to survive the upcoming end of the world due to concerns over the peak oil crisis. In my youth I was so desperate to be the right brand of man that I would seek red flags in fields of green in twisted attempts to prove I was some comical brand of masculine. A would-be Lothario failed only by my lack of desire for any of this to be real at all.

The relationship with the Macedonian model lasted only a few weeks; it fizzled out when she came to visit me in Whitehorse and attended a party I was DJing in someone's basement where we blew the speakers twice and I played Michael Jackson's "P.Y.T." three times in a row because I knew it was Alison's favorite song. I was a little or a lot drunk and forgot I had even played it the first time by the time the needle dropped on round three.

When Alison was away at school and I stayed behind in our five-foot apartment above a garage, I spent hours alone talking to Charlie and playing records, never forgetting which songs I had played but drinking often throughout their playthroughs. In the cold days of the winter, I would make coffee in the hallway kitchen, stare out through the frost growing around the window at a Whitehorse covered in snow and darkened by the lack of sun, and listen to records turn in time on the turntable, my dad's old AKAI table that I had rescued from his basement, long forgotten down there with the other detritus of memories he no longer felt any affinity for.

I will tell you that *Tramp* is a perfect winter morning record for the days that you are feeling something indiscernible in all the bones of your body, tired and weary as it may be. Van Etten's voice chills like a cold wind, beautiful and pained and unforgettable. It shakes and shimmers like a wheel rolling down a road unpaved. Real and tactile like very few things in this world are and all the better for it. Meanwhile pop singers around her became obsessed with the idea of sounding flawless and clean, auto-tuning themselves and their voices to the heavens so they may ascend to some other plane of unattainable perfection.

Van Etten seemed instead to be unable to be anyone beyond herself. Real in the face of so many easy falsehoods. I was easily obsessed. I listened to the National too often when I was deep in my cups because I thought that I must be like these men, broken and sad and longing, and I stopped asking myself whether my desires could live beyond all this. Listening to the National led me to Van Etten when news broke over the digital wires that Aaron Dessner was producing her record, and I traveled down this road to finding her work.

On the AV Club's Undercover series, Van Etten covered the Tom Petty/Stevie Nicks song "Stop Draggin' My Heart Around" with the band Shearwater, and I became obsessed with her on this too. Her raspy voice, her easy confidence, and the way she so effortlessly carries an anecdote at the opening about how Stevie wanted to be a Heartbreaker but Tom (Van Etten jokes at this, saying, "I call him Tom") didn't want her to break up the band, so he wrote her a song instead. I was taken with this person and wondering if I could ever feel so real and self-assured. Less desperate to be perceived as someone but instead relaxing in the comfort of knowing.

In 2011 I was a flickering flame swiftly burning to cinder. I worked alone when it was at all possible, frequently prone to anger and outbursts in the shop, like I had seen emerge from my dad in the past, and I was never able to question why or where from this burning desire to destroy emerged. My dad has always been able to see things in me that I cannot, not full pictures but the hint of desire or the need for change, and an opportunity arose to start my own company—begin my own path.

Where once the plan was to take the seat from him, it seemed now to be a failed project that never fully took flight. Another in a long sequence of misplaced desires that stemmed from my own need to just be someone, anyone, no matter the result. I wanted to be my dad because he was all I could see and it was an easy path of succession. But it was never real, and where I could not see that, he could, and with the notion of starting my own thing on the table, he pushed me to that light instead, hoping to see me flourish somewhere else, somewhere new.

I quit.

I bought thousands of dollars' worth of tools, outfitted my gray 2009 Toyota Tacoma as a work vehicle, and set up an office first at the small table for two that sat by the big picture window facing the world before moving it to a small counter in the hallway kitchen, right by the pantry. I got my first contract, an ongoing project that would take a year to complete at a cultural center being built in Haines Junction, a village an hour and a half drive from my home if the highway treats you well. For the first few days, this felt like my stated purpose. Just as my dad had made his own path in this world, so would I. Never listening to the real lesson of his life but taking what information I could see from it. That I should always do this work, but do it my own way, never asking myself what I need.

Van Etten, on *Tramp*, takes us through the fleeting feelings of a failed relationship that was the source of most of the work on *Epic*, her previous album from 2010. She is singing to and about a man, one who contained the ability to love but never nurture. A wellspring from which pours an endless river of pain that can only ever be filtered over time as it seeks to lose itself in the sea of all things and become forgotten. *Tramp* is beautiful and painful, daring to once again look at the pain of this time that she has moved beyond and sing honestly to the heartache he left her with. Not always to exorcise her own demons but as a means of sharing the hard lessons wrought from trying and difficult times.

She has lived through this, and so can you. She is a dad able to see so much in you that you might miss.

The first day I drove the hour and a half to Haines Junction I left Charlie with Alison's mom, booked a cheap hotel room close to the jobsite, and drove my Toyota down the highway, loaded with a thermos of coffee from the Midnight Sun Coffee Roaster operating out of the back half of a bike shop across from Home Hardware. I drove and scrolled through my iPod tethered by a cable to the stereo that had come with this truck when I purchased it. The massive stereo had replaced the small back seats of the half-cab Toyota right before the truck got repossessed, and Toyota had been unable to sell the truck to anyone due to the overwhelming nature of its stereo and black tinted windows, but I needed a truck, and they were all too eager to sell me this one.

I started a company, opened an email address and printed business cards to give to no one, signed my first contract, and drove down the South Klondike Highway at the break of dawn loaded with tools and caffeine, a dangerously loud stereo blasting indie-folk music.

There is an irreplaceable beauty to the highways in the Yukon; leave a blank section of your life's story where you intend to travel through the north to witness them, even if it is just once. Endless fields of green, amber, and yellow in the seasons that aren't winter, and even in that season the long drifts of snow, the hoarfrost when the weather inches toward negative 40 degrees. Well before cell towers reached out here to these roads, they were stretches of perfect solitude, no one to call, no notifications or urgent emails and requests. Nothing. Coffee staying perfectly warm in a mug in a cup holder, the wind moving around the cab of a truck and music to cover intrusive thoughts.

Driving this highway to the first job that belonged to me, eager to claim some glory in my own name by carving a path that I didn't choose but accepted all the same, my fingers scrolled the dial of my iPod, found the S, turned to *Tramp*, hit play. Let the road throw itself past me as I made turns I knew by heart.

Tramp is Van Etten singing farewells to the pain she's carrying from the failure of a relationship long in the rearview, but trying to find a way to make the canvas more universal, turn the lens outward. Shed some of the pain she's been carrying alone and turn introspection into an opportunity for conversation. In an interview for *The Quietus* in March 2012, Vat Etten told interviewer Cian Traynor, "Even when the story's not mine, it feels like it is when I sing about it. It's learning how to draw that line a little bit, but still putting yourself in there. I feel like if I write from too personal a place, people are going to have a hard time connecting with it. I want to learn to do it on a more universal level."

I was connecting to it, and I couldn't understand why. I just knew it followed me.

Buried in masculine pain all the time.

The first day on the jobsite was spent orienting myself with this new arena of my life. My job was simple enough, long and monotonous and draining but simple. My job was to install every door in the building, a number just shy of three hundred, install every piece of hardware on them, every lock and screw and hinge and door sweep, tighten all the screws, and make sure everything worked perfectly. An impossibly long and arduous process of monotonous rhythms. I claimed an area for myself in the main atrium of the cultural-center-to-be, spent hours stacking boxes and organizing them into a structure that made sense to me, moved steel doors from room to room in advance of hanging them all in their space. My hands were layered in dirt and grime and filth and sweat. I set up my rolling toolbox with everything I needed as I moved from door to door, screws and replacement batteries, water and coffee. A stereo to plug my iPod into for moments alone.

The first week on the jobsite I stayed at the cheap hotel nearby, cheap in appearance but not cost. For $140 a night I had mostly clean towels and a mattress with all the softness of a bag of brown sugar left out to dry. At lunch I would sneak away, buy a Pep 'N Ched and a cup of noodles at the gas station/grocery store, and watch *M*A*S*H* on one of four channels the TV dialed in from whatever satellites were looking down upon us in this land of isolated beauty.

I had never seen *M*A*S*H* but I knew of it. A rare snapshot of an iconic piece of North American pop culture that becomes so omnipresent you never need to actually witness it to know its turns and fables. I suddenly felt alone in a new and very real way. When I had gone out of town on jobs before, it was also as an extension of my dad, working for him, working with him, the successor of my dad's work. Now I was here in a $140-per-night hotel eating chicken ramen out of a Styrofoam cup watching *M*A*S*H*, and I felt terrified and alone and brand new all at once. No supports to prop me up but whatever structures I could create.

*M*A*S*H* became my lifeline to finding some joy in this new life I was building, working alone in the bones of a building with no cell service and the reality of a dream I had been chasing my entire professional career, which was to be left alone. The reality of being alone created a stark and unbearable loneliness. Missing my dad. Missing coming back to the shop after a long day, parking the van inside with him holding the big green bay doors open for my vehicle to pass through. Idle chitchat about what had been accomplished.

I worked long hours on the jobsite alone, trusted to stay safe with the site abandoned and cleared with room for me to carry steel doors by myself from room to room. Transforming the rooms overnight so that every minute when people arrived the building looked brand new. No *M*A*S*H* in here but my iPod on my little stereo, playing the playlists I made that I didn't dare listen to when other hardworking men were nearby.

Sharon Van Etten escaped into her life. The relationship she sings about on *Epic* that features in parts of *Tramp* was one of control, where she felt like she could not be all the parts of her that felt truly real. A singer, an artist, a woman free and in control of her destiny. She drops out of college; she falls in love with a caricature of a rock star boyfriend who discourages her from writing her own music. She struggles; she falls apart. She loses herself. And then, somehow, she finds the strength to fight and to leave. She returns home and crosses the threshold of a family home to rejoin parents she hasn't spoken to in years.

There is a painful lesson in Van Etten's work, a warning of hardship and difficult roads that never try to push you off but rather strongly desire to let you know they exist. That there is something sharp here that might cut you.

I've never been much for lessons. Maybe there's something in the combined measure of my mental illnesses working in tandem, some mechanism of a divergent mind that doesn't let me learn through lessons but rather hardships. Let me always find the stubborn path to achievement.

Play with matches if you think you need to play with matches

"AMY, AKA SPENT GLADIATOR 1"
THE MOUNTAIN GOATS

The first time I tried to quit drinking it was Christmas. Alison and I lived in an old aesthetician's shop that became a home, had moved out of our apartment that was too small for anyone over five feet tall and now lived in an open-concept condo that had floor-to-ceiling windows and hardwood floors. A home built from the bones of what once was a high-end day spa. Our bedroom had been the waxing station; the bathroom was where chemicals had been mixed. It took three days to scrub away the orange stain that had covered every surface, like a vat of McDonald's orange drink had erupted in there and found its way onto every surface.

Alison had been away finishing school in Vancouver when I moved us in. I chose the colors to paint on the feature walls without consulting her, my brash and selfish decisions an unwatched low boil threatening to bubble over and spoil the broth. I hastily chose colors she didn't care for, blue in the bedroom, red in the main room. Trouble everywhere.

It was a small space: one bedroom and a tiny crawl space hiding under it all, where I stashed boxes, old tools, and replacement parts. I built our life in the building before she ever returned home to see it, never gave her space to claim before it was all spoken for. The only thing we chose together was the furniture, choosing IKEA pieces and parts from a great distance, building a cart, building a little life with each click of "add to cart." Malms and Kallaxes and spoons and plates that meant nothing, lifeless artifacts for lifeless times.

I was thirty when we left our old apartment on Eighth Avenue, thirty when I moved us in to this new place. Alison always joked that I had been in such a hurry to be thirty that by the time I was twenty-nine I had already started telling people I had moved into that new decade. For my thirtieth birthday, she organized a city-wide scavenger hunt: every hour I deciphered a clue and moved to a new location in Whitehorse, where a different group of friends were waiting with drinks and activities. Music trivia at Graham's, croquet at the murder basement house, street hockey with cans of cat food in the alley behind the old Food Fair building with Rhiannon and Maciej. It all ended at the Elks Lodge, where I walked into a room full of people dressed like me: pattern button-downs, Converse shoes, people trying to be hat guys, alcoholics. I didn't even notice that everyone in the room had committed to a vibe; it took Alex, Alison's sister, pointing it out for me to notice. People dressed as me, where I had always been dressing like someone I was desperate to hide in. The idea of a man, the shell of a life.

That night I got blackout drunk, took my shirt off, destroyed a cake, fell and smashed my chin on the bathroom sink, woke up in my clothes face-down on my bed. Hid in the shower, where I drank a beer and cried about another decade turning over that was just like all the others, put Irish in my coffee. A theme emerges.

Alison told me in my truck on the way to her parents' house for dinner that she didn't always like some of the music I listened to. The Mountain Goats on my stereo: "Amy, aka Spent Gladiator 1," John Darnielle singing,

I am happy where the vermin play.

She told me she didn't really like his voice, which I totally understand as a critical response. Some voices are not for everyone; she wasn't wrong for not liking it. I stopped playing them in the truck or at home while she was around, one more secret to hide away.

The Mountain Goats are one of those cults you don't even notice you are in despite all the meetings. They were initially a solo project, with John Darnielle recording beautiful songs on shitty boom boxes to shitty cassettes. What flourished through the static and hiss of it all was Darnielle's heart-wrenching and poetic songwriting. Something so urgent that it needed to escape, to be let free. To thrive in the darkest of places. Darnielle wrote about his relationship to addiction, to abuse, to loss, and to failure. But he was always still there singing about it from some triumphant future where he had survived through all the sins of past failings.

People have different entry points to the work of the Mountain Goats, generations granted a piece of culture, each with a pivotal moment soundtracked by a Mountain Goats song to claim as your own. "No Children" in the early 2000s dark-comedy television show *Morel Orel*, "Up the Wolves" on an episode of *The Walking Dead* in 2014, and for me, in 2005, "Cotton" on an episode of the television show *Weeds*.

"Cotton," from the 2004 album *We Shall All Be Healed*, is one of many songs that stray into autobiographical territory on an album that wanders the trails of young addicts. Darnielle was an addict in his younger years. He watched friends disappear and connected dots as the disease came for them, one way or another.

This song is for the rats
Who hurled themselves into the ocean
When they saw that the explosives in the cargo hold
Were just about to blow.

You hear a lot about death when you grow up in a place far away from packed cities filled with strangers who live unknown to each other. Death becomes part of your world; it becomes almost beautiful when it stays still and static. Death is like the hoarfrost collecting on branches in the brief and blinding glimpses of the sun in the midst of a bitter winter. Jane died in the month of May, Tim died that same month the next year. My grandfather drank himself to death, well before he could even meet me. He left me a name, one I would eventually abandon like the ghosts of this place. Death as part of the natural world.

Death, despite the possibility of its beauty, is also a terrifying warning of the dangers of all things. The north, a cold and dark and desolate place isolated from much of the world, suffers from a widespread addiction crisis, and every year I hear the name of a recognizable face who has died of an overdose or by their own hand. The north is a beautiful and wondrous land that hosts a score of problems most will never see until they read the headlines.

Sometimes I wonder where addiction comes from. As if this matters, as if we can trace it back to the source and find the spark that lit a thousand flames and cure all things. Understand the heart of the devil and you may learn to slay him. Sometimes I worry that I spend more time trying to understand why, and less time trying to learn how to keep going.

The Mountain Goats on *We Shall All Be Healed* feel like they're in both of these places, struggling to understand the source and working to keep going. Darnielle has said that not all of his work is autobiographical, but this and follow-up *The Sunset Tree* certainly are. Where *We Shall All Be Healed* touched on young addiction, *The Sunset Tree* digs up the soil of violence at home to see what has seeded there.

Some of Darnielle's most cherished work surfaces here, including "This Year," with its repeated mantra

I am going to make it through this year if it kills me.

Darnielle's determination to triumph despite the hardships laid out around him is an inspiration. In the liner notes of the album, he makes note of his stepfather, the man who, it is heavily implied, inflicted the pain Darnielle suffered at a young age.

On "Hast Thou Considered the Tetrapod," Darnielle sings about vanishing into music alone in his room, avoiding his stepfather sleeping off the effects of alcoholism, safe and free for a moment, and then he is awake, then is guarding his face, then his stepfather's violence.

Held under these smothering waves
By your strong and thick veined hand
But one of these days I'm going to wriggle up on dry land.

My dad never hit me; he has never been a man prone to violence against other people. I am eternally thankful that while in him I saw anger and exhaustion, it was never directed at anyone. I think in conversations about empaths, we see people as soft-spoken, tender wisps and spirits like Counselor Troi on *Star Trek: The Next Generation*. But I don't think that's always true. I think people like my dad are empaths: they feel and absorb so much for the world around them; it's only that they process their emotions differently. With my dad, they explode out of him all at once in a righteous fury, and as a young person it terrified me to the ends of the earth. Never because I thought he would turn the flames toward me, but because I worried I was possessed of the same.

My dad quit drinking before I was born. My mom tells me this story, as she does all our memories. My dad isn't known for telling long tales. They were living in British Columbia and he was working in a glass shop, as he has since he was thirteen. Everyone sat around at the shop after work and drank, went to a second location and drank again. Rinse. Repeat.

One night he came home, slept in his clothes and his shoes. Woke up the next morning and told my mom he was never drinking again. She laughed, so thoroughly used to the rinse and repeat of it all.

He never drank again.

I was terrified of my dad sometimes, but only because I was afraid of the kind of strength that it takes to explode and never destroy. I am an adult writing this book, and I'm considering the weight of so many things that weighed my dad down when I was young and scared and how exhausted he must have been at all hours of all days. Every day he rises; every day he fights to make it through to the next one so that all the people in his life that he cares for beyond measure are able to see a new day without worry.

I am going to make it through this year if it kills me.

Darnielle takes great pains to show us the sharp edge of the world in so many of his songs. The first album I bought by the Mountain Goats was 2002's *Tallahassee*, an album that tells the story of the Alpha Couple, a recurrent theme throughout Mountain Goats works that you would know if you came to the meetings. The Alpha Couple are stand-ins for unhappy marriages, the way being unhappy festers into bitterness, anger, destruction. Darnielle's own parents served as inspiration for the fictional couple's story told through dozens of songs over the breadth of the early Mountain Goats catalogue. "No Children" was the standout track of this era, finding new fans in each new generation that discovers the band, perhaps bolstered by an all-too-real chorus bellowed in Darnielle's wavering falsetto,

Hope you die,
I hope we both die.

This world is not perfect, it will scar us time and again and leave us haunted by ghosts we may never exorcise. We are often toxic people poisoning the soil beneath our feet, destructive masochists who love and yearn and fuck and fail and rise to see new days too. We are complete, we are flawed, and it is in fact our flaws that allow us to be real. Darnielle isn't a perfect guitar player, he is not possessed of a pitch-perfect voice, but he uses what tools he knows and trusts to tell the stories he can, and that is more perfect than a clean pitch or a well-executed chord. Perceived flaws wielded like shields and daggers.

On *Tallahassee*, Darnielle brought in a full band and began to move away from the earlier boombox era of his work. Fans, cultists, and casuals alike mark this period as where the train changed tracks forever. Some prefer to stay where they were; others like the journey into unknown caverns. Some people are both. On *We Shall All Be Healed* Darnielle went one step further: now the band was in a studio with a producer, John Vanderslice, and the Mountain Goats were becoming something more than just Darnielle, a guitar, and a boombox desperately holding on.

A full band allowed Darnielle to not bear the full weight of performance and storytelling and all things. Peter Hughes joined on bass for *Tallahassee* in 2002 and has remained with them ever since. Former Superchunk drummer Jon Wurster joined in 2009 for *Heretic Pride*, replacing a revolving door of fill-in drummers and rounding out a core lineup that has endured to the day I am typing this.

The boombox era feels pure for a lot of people for myriad reasons. It is raw, unfiltered, direct, and powerful. Like a lot of lo-fi art, it is often treated as something pure, made real by the grit and hiss and scratches there on its skin. All of these things can be true, but all of this can be a lie. This is, more than anything, the promise of art. Nothing is real unless you believe in it.

After I turned thirty I thought about my mom telling me about my dad quitting drinking before I was born. I thought about my dad's anger that scared me, plagued my memories. Anger like a whirlwind on fire. I thought about my own anger, my own despair, and the sadness I felt in my heart and head that I couldn't bring myself to tell anyone. I thought about how a friend of mine once called me an emotional robot. I never cried in front of anyone, kept it hidden away like a shameful secret. Never show. Never tell.

I exploded though. I yelled, I smashed things at work, threw tools. I yelled at apprentices for slight mistakes. I had so much anger in me that sometimes I felt like my blood was gasoline and my hands flint and tinder. I was so desperate to be someone, to be some kind of real that felt pure and noble, with scratch and hiss on my skin, that I let the anger consume me all too easily. Never cry, never let anyone in even when they are so desperate to get there. I was intimate only with furious anger. I had abandoned all the things I loved in a desperate quest to be something that people could believe was real. The only problem was that I knew this was all a lie.

When I was a kid I played Magic: The Gathering with some kids from school. We played Magic and talked about starting a Dungeons and Dragons game and traded secrets about video games before the internet existed to do these things for us. We lived in worlds of fantasy beyond the realm of our lives, sheltered away from the world at large that felt bigger than ours.

When I was a kid I got jumped walking home from the comic book shop that used to be in the building next to the old KFC, on Second Avenue just before the Yukon River bridge. I bought some packs of Magic cards, a comic book, a Jolt cola, and a bag of barbecue chips from the Riverside Grocery on the last corner before the bridge, the grocery shop that always smells like homemade soap and sausage from the butcher shop next door. The sign that used to read "Open 24 Hours" when I was a kid that has since been downgraded to "20 Hours" in the intervening years.

I waked home across the bridge, then onto the path that runs alongside the Yukon River, which was worn down by the years of feet making best paths through the trees and the bush. It's paved now, a 4.5-kilometer loop that runs around the river where families walk dogs and young babies in strollers and stop to say hello. As a kid it was wild, overgrown, and private. A place to lose yourself, a place to be on guard, lest the unthinkable happen.

I got jumped there by some kids from school who tore the comic book out of my hand, an old issue of *Spider Woman* from the '70s, the final issue in a short run that had been the first comic I ever read and fell in love with. What was I, some kind of fag? *Spider Woman*? She's supposed to be a man. They tore the cellophane package of Magic cards from my hands as I fell to the ground, threw them to the mercy of the raging waters of the Yukon River. Took the Jolt Cola and the barbecue chips from me as payment for the crimes I had committed. One of them yelled at me about my dad being a construction guy: I should be stronger, too, as he kicked me in the stomach just lightly enough to let me know he could have done it a lot harder if he wanted to hurt me. You gotta learn to be a man too.

I always felt like the Yukon was obsessed with the idea of me being a man, and this led to my obsessions with it too. Addicted to the chase of it. I became ashamed of the things I loved and learned to hide them away. Hide the things that might hurt you; only show your strength and the flames of your anger.

I sometimes forget days and weeks of my youth, but I remember being angry, and I remember being scared.

As the Mountain Goats developed as a band, as a unit beyond just the words and ideas of John Darnielle, the themes they explored opened wider too. Darnielle had worked through so many of the demons of his youth on *We Shall All Be Healed* and *The Sunset Tree*, and now there was so much life left to live, to explore, to unpack and remember. I wonder sometimes if so many people are like me, if they loved Darnielle's music because it reminds us we can keep going without losing all the parts of ourselves that we once loved.

In 2009, the Mountain Goats released *The Life of the World to Come*, an album that explicitly explores narrative storytelling through Bible verses and Darnielle's keen interest in religious themes and iconography. It's the first album of theirs that I skipped and told myself wasn't for me.

Sometimes I wonder where addiction comes from, as if I can trace back to where it began and root out the heart of the devil. I liked to drink because it helped me forget. Abuse anything long enough and it strips parts of you away like wallpaper, sometimes in large pieces, and others in little chunks and particles. The forgetting is a good by-product of the good times and the long nights that become days that turn to nights again without ever sleeping. You drink, go to a second location, drink more, wake up on the floor, search for clues to days and hours.

I avoided *The Life of the World to Come* because I tend to avoid religious themes present in anything, even though I went to youth groups and Bible camps when I was a kid. Even though I briefly loved God and all of his promises, but even then it was only due to being forced into it. I went to the Marsh Lake Bible Camp out on the highway as a kid with Tim and the other kids whose parents attended local Baptist churches. The Bible camp where we played capture the flag, shot BB guns, bought Skittles and cans of Pepsi from the tuck shop, learned all the promises of Jesus. Youth pastors performed skits about the infidels of the world outside and the strength of Jesus to conquer all. Sometimes you don't know you're in a cult despite all the meetings.

It was late at night in the cabin I shared with ten other boys when they discovered that I slept with a teddy bear hidden away in my sleeping bag. A yellow Care Bear that my sister had given me when I was younger. An older boy said that he thought I was gay, and others quickly joined in. The voices became loud, the accusations and the abject cruelty of young people rooting out differences in others to make themselves feel strong. I started to cry, and then sob, and then it was uncontrollable. The voices got louder. A cool youth pastor in charge of our cabin who once caught me singing the song "Shit Towne" by Live and told me it was "cool if I sing that song to myself; just don't let anyone hear you sing the chorus" led everyone in a circle around me. They prayed for me, prayed that I may be fixed, be healed, belong, accept.

A few days later my dad picked me up from camp, drove us home in his white 1988 Chevy S-10, "I Guess That's Why They Call It the Blues" playing on the mixtape in the dashboard. He asked me about camp, and I talked at him about the promises of Jesus. Did my dad even know we were all sinners? Had he been saved? The anger of my father emerged. He yelled, his voice filling the single cab of the truck and drowned out Elton John's voice. He protested the fact that he is doomed to hell simply because he hasn't bought into the promise of a book. I was terrified, and I thought he was mad at me.

For decades I thought he was mad at me.

I drink to forget, and I drink to avoid, and nothing got processed; it all got lost somewhere like loose change and old keys. The reasons behind addiction, the source of anger. My dad was never mad at me. He was mad because he could tell something had changed so dramatically in me, that something or someone or some group of someones had convinced me to be someone I wasn't. It shook anger loose from him like lightning. Mad at what had happened.

The last song on *The Life of the World to Come*, "Ezekiel 7 and the Permanent Efficacy of Grace," is a haunting dirge about a mob enforcer torturing a man out somewhere in the desert, away from people, off the highway somewhere. Torturing him, but the two bonding, a sinister connection born of violence and sadism. Ezekiel 7, the part of the Bible about the end and destruction and judgment of all things.

Haunting is an easy word to describe so much of the work of the Mountain Goats, because I think Darnielle is haunted too, by addiction and loss and time and violence. This is what draws me to his work; this is what draws so many of us. Moths to our own haunted flames.

When I turned I thirty I started to drink more, because I started to take stock of where I had been and where I was going. Thirty was the start of a new decade, the onset of an era we grow up believing is the one where you become an adult, settle down, figure it all out, and grow old. Life ends at thirty-five. These are all things I believed and worried about. Thirty felt like it was too late to change. I spent my whole life wanting to change, but now I needed to forget.

The Mountain Goats released *Transcendental Youth* in 2012, the same year I turned thirty. Written after John Darnielle became a dad, from a stage in Austin, Texas, debuting songs to an eager crowd he promised he hadn't written "doting father" songs. This was a record about Satan. In a blog post titled "Just Under 1,000 Words about Our New Album," Darnielle wrote, "What am I going to do, suddenly start writing songs about cute things instead of songs about how to wrest cries of triumph from the screaming places? Please. May the baby grow up to spit in my face if I should pose that hard."

Transcendental Youth collects stories of people struggling to find where they're supposed to stand in landscapes they feel starkly out of place within. Outcasts, isolated and broken and retreating. Darnielle does many things well, but what rises above all things is his ability to draw and write the broken and sad people of his extended universe with such tactile humanity. The sad and somber tales of these forgotten people feel real and lived in, maybe because he has lived in the same shoes, shared barstools and church basement fold-out chairs with so many of these same people. The people we often lose or forget.

When I played *Transcendental Youth* on the turntable in our living room, which sat on top of a Kallax shelf Alison and

I had bought together against the accent wall painted a red color she never would have chosen, I remembered her telling me in the truck that she didn't like it. I turned it off when she was at home. When she saw me reading comic books on my iPad during rare breaks from work, she asked me why a grown man read comic books, and I put them away when she was around. I started to hide all the things that I liked. Remembered lying on the dirt by the side of the river, Magic cards thrown to the river, comic books torn away. Remembered my teddy bear found in my sleeping bag. Remembered feeling the shame of the things that I loved, how it felt to have someone see you and mock you for it. I drank to forget.

> *Play with matches if you think you need to play with matches.*

I made good money running my own construction company now, and with my newfound wealth I bought high-end alcohol for our liquor cabinet because Alison's mom told us that it was important to own nice things now that we were adults, like expensive alcohols and cashmere sweaters. Every time I drank, I drank to forget, and so all I could remember was that I hated myself, hated the memory of myself I had half-forgotten and hidden away. The shell of a life, the idea of a man. The parts of myself I showed to people that were rejected. The shame.

The whole time Alison and I dated, I had only one tattoo, my tribute to Jane's death on my bicep. She hated it, thought tattoos were tacky. I wore long sleeves, wanted to get more tattoos but never did. I was eager to keep her happy. I spent my money on expensive alcohol; I drank to forget. I stopped engaging, never told her that it hurt me when she told me all the parts of my life she didn't like. I never opened up or expressed myself outside of the anger that emerged from places that surprised me. I drank to forget why I was so angry.

Alison and I broke up in the fall of 2015, the year the Mountain Goats released *Beat the Champ*, a record that on the surface is about wrestling but is really about death and difficult-to-navigate spaces. Tactile songs about the flaws that thrive in people who hurt themselves to live. It seemed funny on the surface to make an album about professional wrestling because it's easy to make fun of professional wrestling, the way it's easy to make fun of comic books or a teddy bear hidden away in a sleeping bag.

It will always feel like a fall record to me only because that is when the album became real and healing to me. When I could play it on the turntable in the condo in the morning when I made coffee just for me, put a little Irish in it just for me, because I didn't have to feel ashamed anymore. I didn't have to hide myself away anymore. When the intrusive thoughts remained and I couldn't remember why anymore.

On *Beat the Champ*, Darnielle sings ballads to wrestlers whose lives have been marked by time. Who have triumphed over abusive fathers or been stabbed to death just outside San Juan. Death is everywhere, but not always sad or somber. "The Ballad of Bull Ramos" is an up-tempo exploration of the slow decay of a man succumbing to time but enjoying the memories of the days in his rearview and appreciating the gifts he is able to give still with his life, even as his body fails him, as he loses a leg, as he becomes blind. Every morning I thought about death, and most nights too. I thought about how I was in my thirties and close to the end now. I would never grow old. I was too angry, too sad, too broken, too drunk.

John Darnielle never wanted to write a doting father record, maybe in part because of his own troubled relationship with a doting father. Instead he raised a thousand lives with each new record, each a new world of characters who were sad and alone, isolated or afraid. Worlds of death, Satan, decay. Terror. But always tactile, always real. Everything here is not afraid to be seen or heard, and this is the mark of a dad more than a father, never afraid to be perceived, show their cards, live without fear of judgment. Darnielle writes and talks and sings about his love and fascination with all things: religious archetypes, Magic: The Gathering, Dungeons and Dragons, death, beauty, love, loss.

The first time I ever tried to quit drinking I was thirty. I told Alison I wanted to slow down, or maybe stop. She laughed, poured another drink of the expensive alcohol occupying our cupboards, and told me, "Don't become one of those people who doesn't drink," and I felt ashamed of that too. The idea of a life, the shell of a man. All the things I was trying to be and all the ways I wanted people to see me, never allowing myself to be real, always trying to be someone perfect. No flaws, nothing tactile.

Never die, never die.

I can't think of floorboards anymore

"DEPRESTON"

COURTNEY BARNETT

My dad taught me to fix. To mend, tape, and glue to hold all our old and broken things together. Never throw anything away. I could fix anything. Even if I had no idea what it was or what its goals or intentions were in this life, I could trace wires and gears back to their source and find the problem. This is what made me good at repairing automatic doors; this built the construction company that I started and ran on my own, doing my best to work myself to death in its name. I wanted every broken thing to be something that could be rendered useful again.

By the time I was in my thirties my depression had become a feral creature, stalking me from the wild undergrowth that had taken root in my soul. Emerging at night to hunt and look for easy prey. My anxious mind never let me sleep and instead offered infinite possibility for worry and staying awake. Who could sleep when there was time left in the day to stare at the ceiling, looking desperately for answers?

I had begun to reckon with the heat death of heterosexual idealism tethered to entering my thirties in the small town I grew up in. Suddenly I had become an adult, and with that came talk of settling into the roots at home. People would ask when I was going to buy a home, find a wife, produce some children. All things that are good and fine for so many, but I just couldn't place myself in the picture they conjured. I felt increasingly disconnected from friends getting older and wanting different things from their own lives, leaving the partying and reckless abandon of youth behind as they moved into the next phase of their lives. I felt unmoored in the wake of their shifting desires, desperately in need of an anchor.

I write a lot about being depressed, and that's because I am often depressed and this is just a natural inclination. Being depressed and anxious is something that felt terrifying at first but slowly became benign over time. Like the broken toe on my right foot that pops out of joint every now and then to remind me that there is still pain somewhere in here, and that it will go away in time. I have always gravitated to songwriters who display and move through their own depressed and anxious lives. Like a lighthouse for those of us at sea in the murky darkness of our own lives, there's an ease to be found in someone shining a light on the dangerous path ahead. Dad rock is a guiding principle more than a sound or a guitar tone. Dad rock is comfort in the darkest parts of ourselves.

Courtney Barnett makes no quarter about her own relationship with depression. In 2022 she made a documentary, *Anonymous Club*, about her time touring after her critically acclaimed record *Tell Me How You Really Feel* and its impact on her mental health. The self-doubt, the exhaustive anxiety, and the dark holes that appear as traps to fall into. From all outside perspectives she was living a life of dreams, a beloved songwriter who had swiftly risen to the enviable status of an indie icon.

Barnett plays guitar like it's a wheel she has just invented, possessed of a tone and style unmistakably her own. Notes emerge from an instrument that feels like an extension of her soul, moving through nerves into wires and ringing out with fuzzed-up splendor. It's a guitar that is matched by her voice, playful and endearing with a little bite and a wink. It's an effortless charm that can only emerge from years spent working on and honing a craft, becoming so in tune with the actions of your trade that it becomes an afterthought, like a breath.

I was good at my job, and this was my constant. I had once been clumsy and unskilled, but over days that turned to months and then years I became good at the work. My dad taught me to be a glazier, and through him I learned how to pick up a sheet of glass on my own, lifting carefully, holding my muscles in the right places to avoid damage and loss of limb. He taught me how to cut a four-by-eight-foot sheet of glass into perfect pieces with nothing but a glass cutter and a spotlessly clean table, how to sand the edges just right so there's no risk of injury. How to find pride in all the little things people will look through or take for granted. No one considers the work that went into making a window, but they are always glad that it has blocked the wind.

I was good at my job, and for a long time being good at my job defined me, until slowly the desire for something more started to eat away at my skin. I wanted all the cuts and scars and sweat of the day to make the hours around it come alive; instead, working long days often dragged into the night. Most often it was me coming home covered in dust and blood, trailing exhaustion and the virtuousness of working so hard I bled behind me through the door. Sometimes my body hurt so badly I could only lie on the floor and let my muscles collapse into themselves while I drank and thought about drinking and ordering takeout. I wondered if they could deliver to me right here, on the floor of a condo I was renting that I would never be able to afford. Everything out in the world was fixed, and I could barely move my body once it hit the floor to rest.

I heard Courtney Barnett for the first time on Prince Edward Island, where my friends Mathias and Ariel had purchased a chunk of property close to the ocean, endless acres of dense forest and unknown secrets, all hiding behind the crumbling shadow of a beautifully in need of repair one-hundred-year-old farmhouse. I had flown out to help them tear down and rebuild, taking a vacation from the labor at home to enjoy labor in the hazy heat of a PEI summer.

We started tearing apart the skin and bones of the farmhouse. Tore faded shingles off the exterior walls, pulled rotten wood and old insulation out from their graves. We worked and sweat out in the heat of the island sun for hours upon hours, Mathias playing CDs from a small stereo tethered to a power cord inside the shell of the house, a portable player that reminded me of the kind you would buy at Walmart for twenty dollars in the late '90s. We played through the hits, Paul Simon reissues with demos and unreleased tracks at the end, Mathias's favorite—a demo of "Rene and Georgette Magritte with Their Dog after the War" from *Hearts and Bones*. I talked about how that song reminded me of my mom, talked through my half-recalled memories of what our home used to look like. Mathias asked if I wanted to listen to Courtney Barnett, and I had to be honest and say I had never actually listened to her. I had seen the name, an article in a copy of *Under the Radar* magazine I read on the plane, but I knew nothing of her work. Mathias, excitedly, ran into the house to put on a CD.

"You're going to love her." he said. "She's like Sheryl Crow, if Sheryl Crow was an Australian lesbian."

Courtney Barnett is kind of like if Sheryl Crow was an Australian lesbian. Mathias put the CD in the little portable player, hit play, and "Elevator Operator" picked up as if the song had been playing for hours already, waiting for someone to find its frequency. Drums and guitar and Barnett's voice all launching into frame at once. I was struck by the casual confidence I heard in her songs, the way her singing felt effortless and trained in equal measure. It became hard to swing hammers and pull boards and nails while straining my ear to listen to verses and phrases. Barnett is like Sheryl Crow in that she has the diorama of a world that inhabits each song, people who move about static backdrops electric with life and possibility.

Born in Sydney, raised on American singer-songwriters before finding herself as an artist, Barnett grew up playing in bands around Australia, first as part of post-grunge band Rapid Transit, then a psych-country outfit called Immigrant Union, before slowly coming into her own voice as a singer-songwriter. Her first EP, *I've Got a Friend Called Emily Ferris*, released on Barnett's own record label (Milk Records, formed with her former partner Jen Cloher), was the emergence of Barnett as a songwriter with a voice and style that was a refreshing change from much of the posturing and excess of mid-2000s indie rock. Barnett as the host of a world built in her work, a songwriter who is shades of whimsical, honest, endearing, and depressed in her creations. Real, tangible. Enviable. Barnett felt whole, like someone who had survived and was here to tell you the pathways back to the source of all problems that she had discovered.

Courtney Barnett's debut full-length record, *Sometimes I Sit and Think and Sometimes I Just Sit*, released in the spring of 2015, is a collection of clever, biting, and insightful songs that feel alive, but the kind of alive that often prefers to be left alone. Barnett, with her laconic, deadpan vocal delivery, is a master of presenting the matter-of-factness of her world as something that is vividly real, colorful, and bright even when it's kind of sad. On "An Illustration of Loneliness (Sleepless in New York)" she wistfully sings to someone she is thinking about as her eyes burn holes into a ceiling. "Nobody Really Cares If You Don't Go to the Party" is the rallying cry for anxious brains everywhere, those who are deciding on outfits and making plans who also would rather just stay at home and put their minds at rest.

Gets harder in the winter, gotta be a fake or shiver
It takes a great deal out of me.

I took great pride in being able to fix things; it often felt like the closest I would come to doing something that would thrive beyond the outline of me. Back home in Whitehorse I had started my own company where I built, repaired, and maintained automatic doors. I was the only one in town who knew their secrets, and even the doors that seemed like they would never open again needed just a few hours on a ladder, some blood and dirt and whispered swearing, and the doors would slide and swing again when it had previously seemed impossible. I was good at something, and it was the only time it felt nice to be alive. I liked being handy, I liked being needed, because I was desperate for there to be a reason why I was even here at all.

Courtney Barnett became an artist that dominated my iPod, every playlist featuring a song of hers, perfectly placed between depressed and melancholic songwriters to act as a pole holding emotional weights. Something in how she approached the world she inhabited with wry grace and cautious whimsy kept her in rotation for me. She's charming, and enough charm can distract from the cuts that appear in the body. Not depressed like *this is the end*, but depressed the way the rain falls too hard and turns the sky off-gray and half-dark.

She builds a world in her songs, like so many great songwriters who are storytellers do. A world that feels tangible and lived in, brick and mortar, sweat and exhaustion. I don't always need music to reflect me, or for there to be some way to feel seen in its gaze, but I appreciate it when it happens. With Barnett, her work feels like it understands work, labor, exhaustion, anxious and intrusive thoughts. It's all there, some songs playful and wired, others withdrawn like a breath releasing the stress of the day. But it's real, words formed from memories and scars. Real in a way you can imagine yourself being real if you close your eyes and listen to the lessons present.

On "Depreston," a portmanteau of both a state of mind and a place to live, Barnett moves through a beautiful and serene backdrop, the soft and gentle strum of her guitar that feels like it conjures sea air, fresh and bright. The gentle timbre of her voice washes ashore like light waves on a perfect morning, gathering sand. Barnett laments looking for a house, for somewhere to build a life in a home that creaks under your feet. Work that needs doing. Move out of the city, stop spending money on lattes and other frivolous attachments of urban decay, and live somewhere affordable. It seems fine; they've got the percolator for coffee anyway. Disconnect from all things, move out to where life offers something new.

When my depression became too feral and too reckless, I made an appointment to see a therapist. I had seen her once before, years prior, sat in an awkward office chair, walked down an awkward hallway, sat in an awkward room, and cried in front of someone for the first time in years. After that I never went back.

She asked me why I came back after all this time. I threw caution to the wind, took my opportunity. This place felt safe. I had cried here before, the awkwardness was gone, and I had very little to lose. I told her, I think I'm transgender.

She looked at me, sitting in her chair in my work clothes, a red-and-white buffalo check work jacket with a burn hole in it from the time stray sparks set it on fire while I was cutting some steel with an angle grinder. My beard, my unkempt hair. My ears covered in blood and dirt. My worn steel-toed Blundstones. I wanted to be a woman?

"Oh we don't use that word, I don't think" was her response. Then she told me that it was a shame someone like me, someone so handsome and young with my life ahead of me, would want to throw it all away like that. But it's okay, she told me. This was just the mental illness talking. I was sick, and all sickness can be cured. I thought about how the last time I was in there I cried about Jane, who had died of cancer, and how "all sickness can be cured" wasn't exactly true, was it? Sometimes things just kill you.

And I can't think of floorboards anymore.

The house they try to buy in "Depreston" shifts in the daylight, as she begins to see the clues that the house is for sale because someone died there. Someone lived all their days there until all their days were over and now it was just the shell of something that used to be real waiting for someone to move in with dreams of an open floor plan and the kind of change that fixes nothing but feels daunting all the same.

I sat in this therapist's office and listened to her tell me that being trans was just a by-product of some other sickness, some kind of depression. Something curable. All things are curable. Wasn't I such a man? They could fix me, you know. She wrote a note on her pad. Cures. I thought about the time I failed French because my teacher thought the word *vegetable* in French was "le vegetable." Not everyone is equipped to do everything. She said she didn't want to do anything extreme, like electroshock therapy, which was good because I hadn't once considered it to be a real or viable option in the first place. Couldn't we talk about it for a while?

She asked me about my goals. Didn't I want to get married, have children, own a home? I should buy a home. Her eyes lit up at the prospect of real estate, and I wondered if she also got a commission if I bought a house on her street. I told her about the time I nearly bought a house years ago, and how it was almost a done deal right until it wasn't. And how it had made me sad. Sad, but not depressed. Sad like when they're out of ice cream at McDonald's. Not depressed like *don't leave me alone near any good jumpable bridges.*

That house became everything to her. This was the source. Couldn't I see it? Couldn't I see how being denied this sort of mark of my masculinity—home ownership—stripped me of my virility? I was handsome, she could see that. "The girls must love you," she said. Didn't that make me happy? No, but that didn't matter either; she was on a roll. I moved from woman to woman because I didn't have a home to keep them in, make our lives together. Have children, grow old, die with dignity. Masculine dignity.

In "Depreston," Courtney Barnett sees the mark of a life that was lived and was lost here more than she can think about moving out to this place and starting a life of her own. The handrail in the shower for a frail hand to use as support, the photo of a young man in Vietnam. Who was this house for, and what mark did they leave behind?

If you have a spare half a million.

I left the office thinking about buying a home, and the electroshock therapy that hung like a threat in the room if I didn't live my life right. She told me to come back in a week; we would work through this. She would fix me. She used the word *fix*, and I thought about how I could fix anything, too, how I could trace the problem back to its source and make anything function just right. How it's supposed to.

I'm ready for both of us now

"WANT YOU BACK"
HAIM

I never liked to dance. This is a lie, but the easiest one to maintain. I didn't like to dance because to dance is to know your body, and I did not want to know my body. It was just a vessel, moving through the world but never comfortable or at ease. A body as a utilitarian object. I wanted to dance, but every time I worried about letting myself go I worried about being seen for something other than the lie I was holding together with tape and best wishes, the way my dad would fix the cable on an old power tool.

I never liked to dance unless someone wasn't looking, and then I danced all the time. I didn't like pop music, either, unless no one was there to hear it and then it was loud and filled every corner of every available room. Then it made my heart soar, my feet create movement they never dreamt themselves capable of.

Alison and numerous other ex-partners found it charming if not annoying that when I would get drunk at parties I became obsessed with the absolute worst pop songs, edging on blackout drunk dancing to "Party Rock Anthem" by LMFAO. Letting myself go, letting myself just enjoy the moment and be free, but only when I was out of control, only when I could mask my joy in dense layers of misplaced irony.

For all the times I was spiraling in endless binges of drinking and partying, I had imaginary lines drawn on territory I would never let myself cross over to. I never did cocaine, never dropped acid or took shrooms. I didn't want to be out of control, I would say. Then I would drink whiskey and red wine until I woke up on an entirely different day than the one I remembered with mysterious blood on my hands. I didn't want to lose control because I was worried I would tell people who I really was, all the parts of me hidden in all the corners of my mind, and to this day I don't actually know if I ever did.

I came up in punk rock, and if you grow up a punk rock kid you have the same imaginary lines drawn around the perimeter of permissible taste. Poptimism wasn't invented until I was old enough to look down my nose at the idea of it. Poptimism is the theory that pop music deserves and has earned the same kind of critical treatment that other genres have been granted. But I came up in punk rock and we like to have opinions about all the things we hate for reasons we can barely articulate and be contrarian, and I would argue that there was no greater champion for the cause of poptimism than HAIM.

HAIM, a trio of sisters—Este, Danielle, and Alana—from California, grew up playing music together in their family cover band, Rockinhaim, with parents Moti and Donna Haim. Their last name stylized into a band, HAIM, and then into a brand. Este and Danielle briefly spent time as members of mid-2000s pop combo Valli Girls before forming HAIM in 2007. None of them took it all too terribly seriously. Just something to fuck around with until it becomes all too real.

I wanted to like pop music so badly, and I envied everyone who did not have the same hang-ups about the most inconsequential shit like me. I don't believe you know yourself fully until you know who you are when you let loose. I am not saying dance like no one is watching, because someone always is, even if it's just you. But I believe we should all know how it feels to be free.

HAIM became real after Danielle spent some time touring as the drummer for Jenny Lewis, which led to her being brought onboard to play guitar with Julian Casablancas, until finally she played in Scarlett Fever, the all-female backing band for CeeLo Green. The taste of possibility in the world lingered with Danielle Haim, and she turned down touring more with Green in favor of corralling her sisters to make something of themselves, together, instead.

Yukon winters are long; they are dark and they are cold and they are crushing. They will kill you if you're not careful, either the physical body or the spirit or both. I grew up with my backyard leading out to the Yukon River, and some days I forgot that I lived in front of a body of water that has claimed the lives of countless people—friends and acquaintances and neighbors—who were pulled into the undertow or walked into its frigid waters when the despair of all the darkness around us became too much to handle.

You need to find a way to survive, and you need to find people to survive alongside.

This is why we drank, because there wasn't much else to do. There's an old bowling alley in Riverdale, across the street from the Sternwheeler Village townhouses, next to where the old Riverdale Market used to be when I was in high school, next to where the gym is now. It looks the same as it did when I was ten years old and our team, the Hot Crabs (I don't know where this name came from), came in second place in a tournament. Hot tip: cheapest beer in town.

There's the skate park, right on the corner before you cross the Yukon River bridge, next to F. H. Collins High School. We used to have a lot of rumbles there late at night, until the one time someone brought a homemade pipe bomb and threw it into the bowl. A guy I worked with at the Food Fair took the blast right in his stomach and had to be taken to the hospital, which was luckily located just up the road and across the street.

Cross the bridge and all that remains are places to get drunk and the memories of places where we used to do the same. In an attempt to contain the spread of rampant alcoholism in the north, liquor laws stipulated that you couldn't have a bar unless it was attached to a hotel. This created an unprecedented era of the worst hotel rooms imaginable. The kind of rooms a corpse wouldn't want to be caught dead inside, sitting on top of the greatest bars of our dwindling memories. The Capital Hotel, long since renovated and gentrified, with its carpets stained by the blood drawn from arguments lost at the business end of a broken bottle. The Taku Hotel for karaoke on Wednesdays and Saturdays, where old cowboys would come and sing Roy Orbison songs to their dates and teach young women how to do a proper two-step. Before the smoking laws changed to ban our habit from happening inside, you could order a pack of Player's Light and a can of Molson Black Label right to your table. Now it's a high-end sports store. The fading memories of good times all washed out in brown liquor.

We invented ways to survive, and all our innovations became parties. A friend who has gone on from the wild years of our youth to become an extremely successful lawyer was the undisputed king of a good time. For years he lived in an apartment above a restaurant that was always changing its name, and with no fear of making too much noise he threw parties that became legends passed along with each new generation of eager partygoers. There was the superhero party, where you had to come dressed as a hero or villain of your own creation and choose an alignment for the midnight superhero battle that found us taking over Main Street. There was the wrestling party in the backyard of the house he lived in the basement of—we dubbed it the murder basement because the morning I helped him move in I could only describe it as looking like a Dexter kill room—where partygoers gathered enough spare mattresses and padding to make a DIY wrestling ring. We somehow made it through that party with a shockingly low number of broken bones. We all chased the dream of a perfect good time, just one more, hoping the next one might finally be the one to make us feel alive. It was so easy to follow this path, lured by the siren song of a promise too perfect to ignore. What if the next time I could fall in love, what if the next party turned the lights on in the darkest nights of the winter? What if I could fix what was so irreparably broken inside me somewhere?

HAIM's first record, *Days Are Gone*, released to critical acclaim in 2013 when the sisters were in their early twenties. The cover of the record finds the three of them, effortlessly cool with standoffish charm, sitting in cheap lawn chairs facing the sun. From the beginning, HAIM proved they were never meant to be drawn into simple categories. A rock band, a pop group, influenced by R&B music and the golden age of '70s classics that they had absorbed from their parents growing up. Nothing to prove, unafraid to show you exactly who they imagined themselves to be in the heat of the moment. Free. Enviably free.

My future lawyer friend loved a party, but very few people saw how it affected him to come down from these highs. The peril of chasing a dream that was never there at all is how it will slowly eat away at you when the spirit of the night has given way to the morning. The winter in the Yukon is cold and dark, and I could see the depression in him when we would meet in the morning at hotel restaurants for cheap breakfasts in desperate attempts to soak up the excess of the night before. Those mornings he was defeated and saddened, and it was a hard juxtaposition with the man I saw come alive at night.

We would DJ parties with the equipment we had scrabbled together, a couple of turntables and a shitty mixer that was sticky with spilled beer, and a playlist of surefire hits that would kill at just the right moment.

We once got hired to DJ all night at a bar downtown, the 202 Hotel, right next to a Greek-Italian fusion restaurant. We were offered a fee of $300 and a $200 bar tab between the two of us for our services, but somehow, come the cold hard light of the morning, we owed the bar $375. We sat with that reality over breakfast, lamented the decisions that brought us here, then turned them into triumphant tales of our spiral into depressive alcoholism. But when my friend was on, he was a neon light for all that was good and possible in this world. The man loved to dance, loved a pop song, and always seemed so capable of being free. I envied him for the fearlessness he seemed to find so easily. A man who knew himself, even in his darkest moments, and was never afraid that any one person might see him for who he really is.

Sometimes parties didn't have or require elaborate DJ setups and endless dance floors; sometimes all we needed was an excuse, a computer, liquor, and someone on the internet guiding the party to what they believed to be a perfect music video on YouTube. This is where I saw HAIM for the first time. I firmly believe that the best genre of music video is "en route." Think the video for Green Day's "When I Come Around" or the Verve's "Bittersweet Symphony" or Vanessa Carlton's "1000 Miles." If all of these artists created the genre, gave it form and possibility, HAIM gave it fresh legs to shake for a new generation with "Want You Back."

"Want You Back" is a perfect distillation of so much of what makes HAIM great, this grand tapestry they have stitched together with all the little threads they took from the music they grew up with, this era of classic rock that moved into their hearts through their parents. *Timeless* is an easy adjective to apply to any music that will survive beyond its years, while what is more important is that we build with the tools and materials that were given to us as we grew, and hope that the splendor of what we create will inspire future generations to create something beautiful using tools worn thin from use.

Some night at some party that I don't remember, someone put the video for "Want You Back" on and every part of me wanted to resist the urge to proclaim my immediate love for it. The movement I felt within me with each step that the three sisters take down a road somewhere in Los Angeles that has been shut down for filming. The little movements they make like journeyman dancers to accent notes and key changes, the choreography, their heads turning and their feet shuffling and kicking. Pop music filtered through rock filtered through a perfect radio station playing nonstop hits in a memory that isn't real. HAIM conjures the memories of how it feels to be young, how it feels to yearn and cherish and regret all at once.

And it may never be enough.

As a trans woman, looking back you eventually come to realize that a lot of the women you yearned for in your younger days were in fact the embodiments of your own desire to be seen.

I thought I had a crush on HAIM, and it's very likely that I did because who didn't. But there was something more, something urgent, something real. I left that party with "Want You Back" lingering in my thoughts, walked alone down streets past bars and where bars used to be. Pictured the steps of Danielle, Este, and Alana down a blocked-off LA street and thought of my own tempo out here in the cold and the dark of the Yukon, my feet making erratic time slowed by alcohol and regret. I tried to play other music on my iPhone, desperate to feel or think of something else. Searched for a new obsession in a playlist of sad songs or secret party favorites and came up with nothing. Just the handclaps and the perfect tenor of the three voices of HAIM working as a single unit. Enchanted by rock music, by pop music, by the fusion of possibility of these two worlds.

I was hounded by the idea of bringing some light into all the places beset with darkness if only I could let myself go for even a single second. Let all the pretense fall away, let all my guards down. Maybe let people see me, really see me, and allow myself to be truly judged by my peers. Maybe then I could be free. Maybe this is how we learn to move on, by accepting that we have failed and we are flawed and that we have to be willing to apologize, to make amends, to tell people who we really are. To tell the people we love why we love them, and why we hurt them, and how we will work to make things better.

And I had a fear of forgiveness.

I wonder sometimes if I was so obsessed with this song because it was rare to hear a woman sing about desire from a place of wanting to change, realizing mistakes. When you grow up in a place so rigidly obsessed with the archetype of gender and expectations, you begin to imagine that all these preconceived notions are real.

Want to change my clothes, my hair, my face

"DANCING IN THE DARK"
BRUCE SPRINGSTEEN

There's a line in Charlie Kaufman's *Synecdoche, New York* that dances on the wind in my head, where Hazel (Samantha Morton) hesitates as she considers buying a house that is perpetually on fire. She remarks to a placid real estate agent, "I'm just really concerned about dying in a fire," to which the agent selling a burning home replies back with earnest resignation, "It's a big decision—how one prefers to die."

For a few years I lived above a haunted electrical supply store nestled behind the Ford dealership on Eighth Avenue in downtown Whitehorse. A two-bedroom apartment with a massive kitchen and dining room, outdated carpet, natural pine trim around the floor, and wallpaper acting as crown molding. It looked like the perfect memory of a '90s Chinese restaurant that never got renovated.

I lived up there alone, alone except Charlie, my gray tabby cat and the last relic of an old relationship who had followed me from apartment to apartment without judgment or questioning. Charlie, who had sat on the passenger seat of my midnight blue 2013 Toyota Tundra as we drove to Toronto and then again seven months later when I gave up and drove back to the Yukon.

This was my third apartment on Eighth Ave, and maybe there was something drawing me to the stretch of road the city never bothered to pave nestled in the shadow of a cliff that threatens to collapse and cover the homes that line its base. A big decision, how one prefers to die.

Late into the darkness of the night I would drink heavily, lie on the floor listening to records until they reached the end of their run and then just the rhythmic thump of the needle hitting the end of its journey. From the shop below, through the sound of the needle and drop of a bourbon bottle on carpeted floor, I could hear the faint sound of a handsaw cutting through wood long after everyone had gone home and turned off the lights of the shop. My landlord told me that the building had originally been a woodshed, and one night the guy who owned the place wrapped up the day, walked out into the woods, all desolate, dark, and cold in the winter dusk of the Yukon, and shot himself in the head. Now he was stuck here in this place, measuring twice and cutting once until time folds in on itself and all things end.

Ghosts never seemed to bother me; in fact I'm of the mind that most ghosts are relatively polite and the only way to ward them off is to signal that you're busy: come back later, come back when I need to be shaken. Maybe ghosts just abide by their own kind and maybe that's all I had become, the ghost of a life spent lying on the floor with a bottle of brown liquor listening to Springsteen records.

For years I had a perception of Springsteen that kept me in the weeds with his work. As a kid I had seen the cover to *Born in the U.S.A.* at my friend Tommy's townhouse in the Sternwheeler Village across from the bowling alley. Springsteen seemed comically American, absurdly masculine. As a kid I formed a lot of opinions about all the things I was unable to comprehend because I thought that having opinions made you older, and if I could be old already in my youth then maybe I could get to the end early too.

Born in the U.S.A. is the quintessential Springsteen record, with its iconic cover and oft-misunderstood ballad decrying capitalism and the American war machine. *Born in the U.S.A.* is the reference that anyone will easily draw when trivia comes calling for an answer, but this was in truth a moment of rebirth for the Boss. *Born to Run*, in 1975, had been the first big commercial success for him and the E-Street Band, a desperate push to become a viable star after *Greetings from Asbury Park, N.J.* and *The Wild, the Innocent & the E Street Shuffle* had not provided enough raw ammunition to fire him into the limelight. *Born to Run* proved the songwriting and world-building potential of Springsteen, this man who could spin themes of the ennui of the exhausted working class, of the kind of desperate love that feels it may crush your tender heart into blackened coal, or into threads of pure silken gold.

Born to Run and follow-up *The River* (1978) cemented Springsteen as a statuesque titan of the possibility of rock music, tender and raw and rough all at once, the kind of man you could love so dearly you might lose all that you are. When you think of the music of dads and fathers, the mind conjures Springsteen before all others, because more than most he is the kind of man you wished had been the one that raised you.

My dad never listened to Springsteen. Like many of the icons of classic dad rock, he was never counted among my dad's collection. I'm certain he knows the hits, because the hits are inescapable, but I never once heard the Boss's voice filter out through the foam of my dad's headphones. Springsteen, this voice and champion of the working class, never appeared in my working-class household. I sometimes wonder if this is all by design. Both of these men, Springsteen and my dad, teaching me to defy the expectation of preconceptions.

Springsteen is a collection of fables and stories, the did-you-knows that obsessives trade between themselves like precious currency. Did you know that "10th Avenue Freeze-Out" is about how the E Street Band formed (Springsteen is Big Scooter; Clarence Clemons is the Big Man)? Did you know that "Bobby Jean" is supposed to be about Springsteen's relationship to Steven Van Zandt?

Springsteen is the perfect idea of a man who is both comically masculine and as queer as a three-dollar bill. A voice like a wild animal backed into a corner that drips still with honey and lavender. There is a sweetness to his vision of the world, that all things are rough and the weight of the world a burden few shoulders can bear and yet there is love and yearning and desire amid all the hardships. Springsteen never promises that life and all things will be perfect, instead that there will be loss and heartache and you will love and you will lose but you will find the strength to go on.

I never appreciated how much my dad has always been able to see me, and maybe this is in part because he has kept so much of himself private for so long. He is a man who shares only what he likes, when he chooses, and even writing about him here I worry about ruining the mystique a little. It's not a desire born of secrets and mischief; I have always just known my dad to be unbothered by outward perception or judgment. My dad's love language has always been direct action over words or easy tenderness. He will always be there to show you—even if the words never leave his mouth—that he loves you, that you're safe with him looking out for you.

By the time I moved into my apartment above the haunted electrical supply store on Eighth Avenue, I was tired from shuffling my body along a path going nowhere. I had folded my construction company, moved to Toronto, moved back from Toronto, took a job as a locksmith, hated working as a locksmith, hated myself for moving back from Toronto. Tired. Sad. Eyes sinking into the skull in preparation of closing for good.

There is no coffee in the world that tastes as good as a cup my dad can make. We can use the same beans, grind them to the same grit, and filter the same water through them into a porcelain mug, and I will never re-create what he is capable of. I would sit at the counter in their house and have coffee, and every so often my dad would tell me he could see this work was making me unhappy, no judgment or urging in his voice but just letting me know he could see the weight that slumped my shoulders ever forward.

I never asked my dad what he thought I should do, just always brought my problems and burdens to the counter in their kitchen, a solid white kitchen island in the middle of an open-concept floor plan. I have been eternally blessed to know I can always come to this space free of judgment and say as much or as little as I need to feel heard, to feel safe.

Springsteen wrote *Nebraska* differently than he had previous records, taking time in private to craft his work away from the bustle of a studio filled with external voices and additions. It was recorded at home, with minimal instrumentation captured on a four-track recorder. This is the turning point in Springsteen's work. *Nebraska* focuses on the outward stories of blue-collar workers and dreamers pushing the needle to survive. Working-class, struggling, scheming, and fearful people. It is often cited as an underappreciated gem in Springsteen's catalogue, if only because it was a rare moment of him letting down his guard and laying bare the bones of his work.

I was always afraid, and fear will lead you into dark corners and sad places if you let it. Fear will hold you there until it has drained all that you are. I had tried to come out three times before, and each time it had been rebuked and I had internalized that this was a failure on my part. I had failed to be strong, failed to be bold, failed to be who I thought I might be capable of becoming, and now I was getting old. By the time I moved into my apartment above the haunted electrical supply shop I was in my mid-thirties, and life had told me time and again that your mid-thirties are the point where anything you dreamed possible becomes just an opportunity you have already missed.

The day I moved into my apartment my bank account was frozen by the Canadian Revenue Agency. I had been accruing debt at an alarming rate over the last decade, and my taxes were too much to pay. I owed too much and had too little and so the bank froze my accounts, what money I had went to the CRA, and I had to ask my mom for enough money to pay the first month's rent, damage deposit, plus a box of mac and cheese while I waited for my situation to sort itself out. Debts no honest man could pay.

When I moved into the apartment above the electrical supply store, I knew almost immediately that I would become just another ghost haunting a house hidden at the base of a cliff. I knew I was going to die here. I had dreamed a thousand possible lives for myself in all the years before this one, and they had never once come true. I was so tired of dreaming and turning up nothing. I opened my construction company again, took on contracts and started to bring in some work, enough to make adequate money to start surviving again. I bought tools and food and a gun that I hid in my closet, and I thought a lot about death.

Maybe that was the real ghost of this place, the memory of the end. But I have always lived with intrusive thoughts and I have always dreamed of death, and for a long time I thought this was the place that dream would become real, the final dream I had left to realize after all others failed to come true. At night I lay on the floor, got drunk alone and cried, thought about my failed dreams, and listened to Springsteen records.

Born in the U.S.A. is about many things, but it is more than anything about defying expectations. Maybe that isn't true, but drunk on the floor in an unrenovated '90s Chinese restaurant, it felt like an album that defied possibility.

As a kid I had believed Springsteen to be the patron saint of men I would cross the street to avoid interacting with, and maybe this is the deceptive wonder of the iconic Annie Leibovitz photo on the cover, Springsteen with his back turned, a red hat in the back pocket of his well-worn jeans, and the red and off-white stripes of the American flag in front of him. In contrast to previous album covers, stark photos of his face on *The River* or him playfully leaning on his lifelong love, sax player Clarence Clemons, on *Born to Run*. This was the first time he was on the cover but still unseen, a man walking away, or perhaps toward something, but asking you to question why.

When he started working on the songs that would become *Nebraska* and *Born in the U.S.A.*, Springsteen was in his early thirties. In his thirties and still desperately searching for something to define him, to bring him to that next and final stage, the quest for a big enough spotlight to feel seen in the heat of its brilliance. *Nebraska* became a brooding and pensive masterpiece, and *Born in the U.S.A.* a triumphant demand to be heard, to be loved, to be more than anyone believed him possible of creating.

In my thirties in my two-bedroom apartment, I slipped into the hardest moments of alcoholism. I took a part-time job as a bartender at the cocktail bar down the road. A building with two taxidermy moose on the roof, their horns locked in false battle. A fun bit of trivia that we would dole out to tourists taking endless photos of them was that the bodies were actually cows. Everything is a lie, posed and on display. My rallying cry as a bartender was that all shots were whiskey, shots I would eagerly down myself as others did, too, and when I wasn't working I was drinking, and when I wasn't at the bar I was at home, and when I was at home, I was drinking too.

I stopped believing anything new was possible. I was the same person all the familiar faces drinking at the bar or seated at tables around the room had always known. A kid who had once been awkward and shy in high school and my teen years, who grew into a man, handsome enough and pleasant enough and charming enough. At any given time I had likely slept with at least one person in the room, and some of them had names I couldn't always remember. The black holes burned into my brain by years of abuse and brown liquor.

I was dead inside, but I could make a mean old fashioned and do endless shots of whiskey, and maybe this was my lasting legacy. Not much, but at least it was nothing.

Some nights, though. Some nights I wasn't lying on the floor. Some nights something in me moved and shook and I would put records on and shuffle my feet around the house in an attempt at dancing. I would go out on my patio and smoke weed and cigarettes and drink and stare into the sky looking for nothing and think for just a moment that maybe this is just what life was. Sad and dark but there was time to dance still. Some nights I thought about the gun hiding in my closet. A big decision, how one prefers to die. Some nights I would just breathe out, deeply, and watch my breath turn to smoke in the air and think about nothing for a second. Some nights I was free. Some nights I was alone and when I was alone I could be anyone for seconds that threatened to become hours.

I wasn't treating anyone terribly well, least of all myself. Distant to most or putting on airs of overconfidence and determined heterosexual masculinity. I owned a construction company, I owned a truck, I had scars from years of injuries, I had sore muscles and a bad back. In the winter the year after I moved into that apartment I slipped on the ice at the dump and impacted my tailbone, forcing it up and to the left, where it moved into the space occupied by my hip bone. Some days it became too painful to stand up. Painkillers. Booze. Darkness.

Some nights Springsteen records were the only thing saving me. My failing relationships, the piles of debt, the going nowhere of it all. In August 2017 I took the gun out of my closet and sat with it on the bed, and wondered what would happen afterward, when this was all over. What happens after we die. I thought about all my friends and family and former lovers that had died and would I see them somewhere beyond all this? Would they remember me? Would they want to see me? Would I be like this, in this body? Could I be remade? Springsteen playing in the living room on the record player.

Want to change my clothes, my hair, my face.

That line in "Dancing in the Dark" followed me from room to room. Springsteen didn't even want that song on this record. Did you know that? Little facts trading hands. Springsteen had fought so hard to make this goddamn record. Legend has it he wrote fifty to one hundred songs around the period of *Nebraska* and *Born in the U.S.A.*, and the producer goaded him for one more hit and he just kind of lost it. In *Glory Days*, Dave Marsh writes that Springsteen was pissed off at the urging to write one more solid hit. "I've written seventy songs. You want another one, you write it," Springsteen said, stormed out, walked back in, and wrote one of the greatest songs of his career. He was just mad enough to make something beautiful.

"Dancing in the Dark" is a snapshot of loneliness and isolation. How we rebuild ourselves in these moments. Springsteen was in his thirties now, and struggling to continue to be the kind of man that he had been all the years prior to this one. *The River* had been a great success, and Springsteen was starting to feel isolated by the success, by the pressure of expectation and the performance of Bruce Springsteen over the reality of the man.

Radio's on and I'm moving 'round my place.

"Dancing in the Dark" is a pop-rock masterwork, that something so simple could move you to an endless well of emotions. The keyboard droning on in simple rhythms, Max Weinberg's drums hammering out an easy beat, each bounce of a stick off the snare pumping blood into a tired heart. Springsteen sounds exhausted but hopeful, yearning and lost all at once. Struggling, but joyous. Determined.

Hungry for action.

It almost feels like a joke. The Brian De Palma music video where he pulls a young Courtney Cox on stage to dance with him, a somewhat staged moment that Springsteen didn't know was fake and Cox didn't know was real. Springsteen could so easily fall over earnestness into something cheesy and unfulfilling. But there's something in him, the raw determination in the sway of his voice, that moves you to believe there is a life here to hold on to.

My dad has never liked Springsteen, and so I cannot filter it through him or claim some lesson passed from the Boss to my dad to myself. My dad has been a hardworking man his whole life, self-determined, driven, desperate, hungry, tired, bored, isolated, angry. But above all things he has desired a life for himself that feels real, that feels earned, that feels like his. And this is a theme that emerged from "Dancing in the Dark" that felt real to me, too, this desperation for a life to feel real.

I used to want that.

If you don't believe your life can change on a dance floor, I believe you are lying to yourself. Halloween of 2017 my then partner and I were going to different parties, and in a last-minute quest for a costume to hide my body and my alcohol I dressed in a shark costume, put a blazer over top, and filled my pockets with fake money: loan shark. I drank a half-bottle of cheap scotch at home, filled a flask with whiskey and a plastic bag with cans of cheap Pilsner, and went to a party.

That night I danced and snuck booze under my costume, did shots in the kitchen, did drugs in the garage. I went to the bathroom and swayed in the mirror trying to find my reflection and mouthed the words "fuck you" to the face staring back through me from the mirror. The DJ played the hits, I danced a little but could never find the rhythm, and then someone played "Dancing in the Dark" and I felt an overwhelming sense of bitter sadness, as if I had been struck by a lightning bolt of depression. I snuck out, walked home in the winter wearing a shark costume for warmth, drank bourbon and whiskey and told my partner to leave me alone, and fell asleep on the floor with the rhythmic thump of a needle hitting the end of its run.

For days I drank alone, went to work for a few hours, came home, drank. Floor. Drink. Floor. Floor. End of the loop. The rhythmic thump of the turntable, the ghost downstairs, and the end of life. I thought about all the times I had tried to come out and been rejected. I thought about the life I thought I could never have and how all of my time was gone. My intrusive thoughts. I thought about death. Death. Death. Death.

I sat on the bed with a gun and thought about what happens next, and somehow in all of this I decided instead to drive myself half-drunk to the hospital and told the admissions nurse I was in pain, could someone see me. My doctor happened to be the one on call, and through it all I think he could see me, too, and he told me he would keep me there for a few hours for observation.

I went home. I bought a double Quarter Pounder meal with a large fries and six-piece McNuggets, lay in the bathtub with them and a bottle of bourbon, played Springsteen on the stereo loud enough so the words could reach me no matter how far I ran from the truth, and stayed there until the water ran lukewarm, then cold. Charlie came in searching for fries, his special treat. I remembered how every time I came out to someone they rejected me, and so I texted my partner and asked her to come over so we could talk, and I planned to tell her my truth, the truth that had pushed so many away, and then like a coward I could be free and then I could die and all this would be over.

Want to change my clothes, my hair, my face.

She came over, and I stared into my feet and told her I had dysphoria. Gender problems, you know. I don't want to be this anymore. I prepared myself for the pain, knew it; it had been so long I almost craved how it felt. Like getting a tattoo after an absence of fresh ink. I never expected her to say what she did, but bless her for doing so.

"Okay, so what do you need that will help?"

I was never prepared for this, what happens when you fight hard enough for what you really want and it ends up becoming everything. We went to Walmart, I bought shitty clothes that didn't fit right, I bought shaving cream, I shaved my beard and the hair on my body, and I checked my look in the mirror. I drank and shaved and drank and shaved, and with each pass of the razor a face emerged and I changed, became something new. I had thought I was so old and so tired and so done, and yet here I was, changing. Possibilities emerged. Something and someone new. The Boss sings in the living room. Messages keep getting clearer and I can hear what he's been telling me all this time, what my own dad has been showing me all this time.

It had been so long since I had really, truly chosen. But here I was, shaving possibility into my face, and for the first time I felt like I could see a way forward. Break out of isolation, move beyond all this. The lesson of my dad, of so many who tried to raise me, and the hidden beauty of a perfect Springsteen song of naming and announcing not only all the things haunting you but also the desire and need for that single spark to ignite your life.

Pick up the pieces and go home

"GOLD DUST WOMAN"
FLEETWOOD MAC

I never knew that I was leaving; with each turn down every street I had no idea that this was my farewell tour. There was a time when only a few people knew that I was trans. I told my partner at the time, and then the office manager at the place where I had taken a temporary job as the executive director of our local music industry association. I told our summer employee after she wondered why I shaved my beard off and started wearing high-waisted black Levi's, a black shirt, and black paint on my fingernails. She just thought I had gone goth, which somehow seems like a harder vibe to shift into in your mid-thirties than coming out as trans. I wasn't going to tell my family.

We didn't really talk about this sort of thing in my family. We told stories long after the dust had settled, but never really discussed things and changes in the moment. Some things are private, some things we hold deep inside ourselves somewhere. My mom always tells me about my dad's brother who was gay. He died when I was very young. There's a single photo of me sitting in his lap that used to be in the big cardboard box of photos my mom kept in the back of her closet that my sister and I would sift through on occasion. My sister will remind me of all my memories; she's always had a clearer mind for this stuff. I just let everything sift through the holes I've burned in my mind. Sometimes I wonder what it would have been like to grow up with a gay uncle who could give some kind of guidance. Would I have lived differently? What does it really matter? The dead owe us nothing. They're just there to remind us that something different was possible.

My sister used to speak for me. It took longer than normal for me to even start talking at all. I'm not sure if I just had no use for it or if it was easier to have someone else communicate my needs, but she would act as the go-between for me and my parents. Niko needs food. Niko needs to use the washroom. Niko is sad.

I learned to express need and desire through music. We always had music in our house in the years of my youth: my mom would vacuum and listen to Neil Young's *Harvest*, or bake in the afternoon with the sun appearing in the darkness of the winter, bringing natural light down through the skylights into our kitchen, and play Dwight Yoakam records and tell me all about how he had never been accepted in Nashville so he went to LA and played punk rock clubs instead. She would tell me stories about the time she and my dad saw the Rolling Stones play a show in Vancouver, where the surprise opener was Stevie Wonder. She and my dad both ended up at the same Black Sabbath show once without knowing the other was there. There's something charming to me about my parents both being at a Black Sabbath show, envisioning them with Ozzy in the backdrop biting the heads off bats or doves, seeing each other across the room. "War Pigs" plays.

We talked through music, and this is where I learned to share stories. This is where I learned about communicating, with a record in the background.

My mom got sick when I was thirteen. I didn't really understand it then; it's hard to comprehend that your parent is unwell and that they're not getting better. They're not going to die, but they're not ever going to be the kind of infallible pillar you imagine your parent to be. My mom has Crohn's disease, got sick in the mid-'90s when they knew less about the gastrointestinal system than they do now, and it has given her a harder shake at life then she ever deserved. I have grown up watching my mom become someone who needed help in a family that does not like having to ask for it.

My mom worked at the toy store and the shoe store in the Hougen Centre, then worked at the Coast Mountain Sports across the road on Main Street. Then she had to start taking time off work to be in the hospital. Then she just wasn't able to go back.

We're not obsessed with work in our family, but we are a working-class family and there is a feeling in all of us that we should be doing something. Something in your bones or burrowed there under the skin that picks at you when you're not being productive. I'm not saying this is healthy, but it is how we operate. We don't relax easily, don't like to sit still and idle. I think it must have been hard for my mom to slow down, then to stop. To not be able to have a job to go to. Stay home.

So, she started baking more, even as she was unable to eat most of what she was making. My mom always tells me that her mother wasn't a good cook and that she had to teach herself. You will find no better baker or cook than my mother, a woman with an otherworldly sense of taste and flavor despite the fact that she is unable to eat most things. She just knows what you need; it's baked in there.

She listens to music when she bakes, and so I would always sit at the counter and listen to music and stories with her because when I was thirteen I didn't know if she would ever get better and I wanted to have memories to hold on to. I have never, to this day, grown out of this habit. My mom forgets that she has told me a lot of things; her memory isn't as good as it used to be, and we share this trait but for very different reasons. I hear the story about the Rolling Stones and Stevie Wonder every few months, but it never gets old and I will miss it when it goes.

I was never going to tell my family.

There are certain songs that draw specific memories on the white board of my mind. The Traveling Wilburys remind me of the purple Volkswagen Westfalia my parents bought in the '90s that we took on road trips south into British Columbia. Where I would sit in the back on the bench seat that folded out into a bed next to the mini fridge and the little sink and think that this was luxury. What opulence. The smell of the fabric in that van, dust and mountains and fresh air all at once mixed with polyester, stings my nostrils still whenever I hear "Congratulations." My mom telling me about each member of the Traveling Wilburys and how they were never as good without Roy Orbison.

My parents didn't always agree on music. Like all couples who have spent their lives together, there is always something to disagree on, and they have their own favorite lanes. But all roads have to cross eventually; intersections on Paul Simon and Fleetwood Mac create cohesion in my parents' disparate playlists.

This is not uncommon. If you grew up with parents who had a record collection, the odds are in your favor that somewhere in the stack there's a copy of Fleetwood Mac's *Rumours*. Lucky ones had the self-titled record and have the same reaction as I do whenever they hear "Rhiannon" and are instantly transported back to a time when the living room carpet was orange shag and everything was tinted amber and brass. "Say You Love Me" reminds me still of watching the snow fall in the early winter, seeing it collect and pile onto itself on the patio looking out over our backyard, before it had a fence and it was just an open view right to the woods and the river.

Fleetwood Mac has one of those stories everyone knows, but sometimes they forget they've told you this one before. *Rumours* is a legend on the map of the band's legacy, the markers by which all the lore is measured and tracked. A boon for all who love storytelling through the music lingering in their memories. There is so much to cut your teeth on in the story of *Rumours*, told by someone's mother or someone's father or sometimes both, maybe some burnout uncle who made you a mixtape and snuck a prerolled joint into the case. My mom told it to me, as her hands made scones half from memory and half from a faded recipe torn out of a long-lost cookbook in the kitchen with the sun shining down through the skylight.

She told me how the band had gone through so many lineup changes over the years, how sometimes people forget that they're British. Like my dad; people sometimes forget he's from Wales because he doesn't strike you as Welsh. But that's where he's from. She sidetracks to telling me once more that my grandfather flew for the RAF in the war, then came to Canada when it was all over. How he opened a glass shop there and the whole family lived above it.

She told me about John and Christine McVie. They were a couple, but they had this spectacular breakup before they made *Rumours*. And then there was Lindsey Buckingham and Stevie Nicks. They had this intense on-again, off-again thing that was really kind of a mess. She has a voice that will just stop you dead in your tracks. Then there was Mick Fleetwood, who divorced his wife because she had been cheating on him, even though I'm sure he was fooling around on her the whole time too. It's all just this big mess, but they still had a record to make. They only ever got along when they were working on something, and they made this beautiful portrait of a group in turmoil, *Rumours*.

Listening to my parents' copy of *Rumours* on the stereo in the corner of the living room was how I did my best to understand them, where they came from, what they were saying when all things were silent. *Rumours* is the memory of a house that might never have been real, stories I've heard before and will hear again. A telephone still tethered to the wall by a cord and the door that used to be at the front of my house before my dad took it out and covered it over because it was an annoying spot for a door anyway. My bedroom upstairs, an old bathroom, an old kitchen. Old lives.

The Fleetwood Mac story often feels like it starts at *Rumours*, despite it being the band's eleventh record. That fact will shock people if they didn't hear it from their mother at a kitchen table somewhere. They shifted and changed over time; members came in, then left when the music or the world around it became unrecognizable to them. They are remembered as this classic lineup, the one heard on the self-titled record and then *Rumours*, followed by *Tusk*, a record that people will sleep on because your parents told you it's weird, but that's only because it is weird and that's the best part of it. On *Tusk* the band got a little too into post-punk and experimental music, and it seeps into everything to make a record that sounds like the exact sort of thing you would create to shake off the weight of *Rumours*.

As a dad rock band, they become the opening promise to dad rock being more than just something tied to tired gender archetypes. Dads are not always men, and dads are not always fathers. Dads are simply there to raise you as best they can with the lessons and failures that have carried them far enough that they can look back and help you build a world to grow old in with stories they might forget they've told you before but will share again all the same. They will entrust you with beautiful melodies that will conjure flashes of a time that seemed easier only because you no longer have to live in the moment of how hard it felt then.

I was never going to tell my parents I was trans, but I shaved my beard and it was alarming how that simple act of personal grooming was enough spark to start innumerable fires. Friends demanded to know what was wrong with my face—many had never even seen all of it. My mom, who had many times in my life protested my facial hair decisions, asked why my look was changing so drastically. I was never going to tell my parents. But my mom seemed confused and I was driving her to an appointment with her doctor at the hospital, and I thought it was cruel to hold secrets from her and so somehow I found it in me to open up. We are not a family that talks about things such as this, but I told her my own story.

I am uncomfortable in my body.

Okay, that's not entirely right. I was trying to not just say transgender because that felt shocking somehow. The truth like an earthquake that might level all things. Take it slow, start with the early warning signs and ease into the moment when all things shake and change forever. She told me she got it, that she didn't like her body either, really. I got forceful then: no it's not like that; it's not just that I don't like my body, it's that it's the wrong one. Not blurting out the truth was proving clunky and awkward. We were standing in the doorway, and she was getting her clothes on and herself ready to go. I was wearing jeans I bought from the women's section at the Joe Fresh in the grocery store. Mom, I'm transgender.

I am eternally grateful I will never have to say that sentence ever again. She was confused, and this is fair because this news was confusing. I was in my thirties, I seemed solidly heterosexual if not a caricature, and people always told her that I was handsome. Wasn't I so handsome? Women seemed to like me, so how come they never stuck around? I told her I was trans and she asked me what about my girlfriend and I realized I did not want to stand in the foyer of my childhood home and explain lesbians to my mother, so we got in my truck and drove toward the hospital.

Well, your dad had a gay brother, she told me. Yes, Mom, I know, this is kind of like that but also very different. She was going to have to wrap her head around this news. Would I like it if she told my dad instead of me, she asked me in the truck as we neared the hospital. I know you two haven't always had the easiest time. I never knew what she meant by this. It felt cryptic, like a story we had both forgotten to tell. I said sure, tell Dad for me. Let me know what he says. She was still in shock, got out of the truck and walked to the hospital for her appointment, and I drove away wondering if this was all over.

I called my sister on the Bluetooth stereo in my truck, a 2013 midnight blue Toyota Tundra on which I owed payments I could no longer afford. She was just about to jump into a meeting, and I told her I was trans so she could hear it from me before Mom called and did her best to explain a concept she had yet to fully understand herself. My sister was mad, but only that she was just about to jump into a meeting and I dropped this in her lap. How am I supposed to concentrate on whatever bullshit ski hill thing is going on today? she said with a laugh, a laugh like she was doing her best to let me know she was okay with this.

We hung up; she had to go to her meeting, and I had to go to work and cosplay as a man who fixed doors around the city. I thought about the idea that she could have had a sister this whole fucking time. What we had both been robbed of, what could have been. Maybe this is why she was always so good at saying what I needed; we were connected in this way, and it's only that I grew up pretending to be someone I wasn't and shut myself down that we lost that tether.

I sometimes wonder if every generation loves Fleetwood Mac because it allows us to claim a new relationship with our parents, gives us some new frame of reference and understanding. Bridging a gap you can't even see between youth and new adulthood. In my twenties I became a bit obsessed with making mixtapes and CDs that included music I thought my parents would like, so they could have something I had made that showed that we were connected, that I shared this lineage they had of music and storytelling and the communication of all things.

It's the mercy I can't take

"SONG IN E"

JULIEN BAKER

Everything has an ending. We are not here forever, nor are we supposed to be. These places, these lives, the memories in the streets and the blood of the places we claim for ourselves. They're not always forever. It's hard to admit when something is over, harder still to understand you simply have no other choice. Life will tell you when it's ready to wrap things up. My life had an ending.

When I was in my twenties and into my early thirties, I saw my life ending when I was old enough to still be young but only just. I saw myself dying when I was thirty-five, thirty-six if I was lucky. Just old enough to have my death not be tragic, but young enough for people to remark that it was still too soon. The sweet spot of finality. People always talk about the 27 Club, the deaths that came too soon: Cobain and Hendrix and Joplin. Few talk about the thirty-fivers of the death world; there's nothing tragic or sexy and alluring about dying the same year you're supposed to start talking to your doctor about yearly physicals.

I drank because I was bored, and then I drank because it was social, and then I drank because I loved the promise of a perfect party, and then I drank because it was all there was left, and then I drank because I was sad. I drank because I was obsessed, and I drank because it helped me forget, and it helped me convince myself that I was not to blame for all of my problems and failings, that I was unable to take any ownership of the situation. Powerless in the face of all these hardships and downfalls. Drinking had pushed all the moments in my past that shamed me away to some forgotten corner of my mind, but it had left behind the scuff marks of their psychic damage. For a long time I couldn't even remember why I was more afraid of God than the devil.

There's a video I return to often when I need to feel devastatingly sad. I think a good cry is a healthy part of your day, like a fresh grapefruit or a careful stretching of your muscles. The video is Julien Baker, playing a black piano on a stage in Brussels in 2016. She opens the song gently, softly speaking into the microphone aimed at her face, "This is for my new friend, Tom." She brushes her hair away from her face and sets into a stunning and emotionally crippling cover of "Accident Prone" by Jawbreaker.

I think to have a great cover you need to find something in the voice of the original that speaks to something inside you, something that has clung to your bones like barnacles to a hull. Think of Leonard Cohen's "Hallelujah" and its myriad covers in desperate search of connecting to something within

Cohen's classic and oft-misunderstood song. Jeff Buckley and John Cale have certainly had their moments with it, but it's k. d. lang who always feels to me like the strongest connective thread to the spirit and weight of the original, while simultaneously bringing their own spirit to it. People think "Hallelujah" is about many things, and it is played in a dizzying array of inappropriate settings: weddings, funerals, children's choirs singing in church at Christmastime. But k. d. lang, perhaps because they and Cohen both shared a practice of Buddhism or some deeper understanding of spirituality and love, is the voice who always seems to understand the crashing waves of the song. Knowing where it needs to soar into the heavens and understanding just when it comes wafting down to bed. There is something tender here, something sad, something joyous and something that speaks to love, rebirth, survival. All things. k. d. lang gets it. And I dare you to listen to that song and not be overtaken with the beauty and wonder of this world.

Julien Baker similarly burrows to the heart of "Accident Prone," the Jawbreaker song from *Dear You*, released the year Baker was born, 1995. A sublime song about a cycle of self-destruction, self-harm, destroying the body and the soul, the desperate search for love, and the denial of our own self-worth. Denying yourself that you deserve this, have earned this. In Jawbreaker's hands, it's easy to misplace this song as bordering on emotionally manipulative, the cliché of being so broken that how could you deserve to be loved? With Baker and her hands on a piano in Brussels decades after the song was first released, there's something more. The abject darkness of the loathing that leads the soul to this well, the darkness we can fall into far too easily, and how it is so much harder to climb out than it ever was to fall in.

I got to you, there was nothing left.

I thought I would die simply because there was no future to imagine. I had fallen so deep into the well and couldn't see a means of climbing out. Saying that I was sad felt like describing tap water, a natural state that you take for granted is always there. I became obsessed with death, wondering what would happen when it came for me. Every year brought me one step closer to the answer. When Jane died I wondered if she was in heaven, if she was watching the people in her life that she loved: her parents, her brothers, the bull mastiff puppy she had adopted who she never got to see grow old alongside her. I wondered if she would be happy to see me, or if she would still be mad that I never came to say goodbye before the cancer came for her that one last time. I thought about my childhood best friend, Tim, who died the year after Jane had. Would we talk like old friends, could we still reminisce about sitting on the floor of his bedroom playing *SimCity* on the Super Nintendo and his brother telling us about Candlebox? I thought about Ryan, the kid my dad coached in cross-country skiing who died one day at school when his heart gave out doing the twenty-minute run. We were never close, but we had been friends, and would that be enough? Would we just say casual hellos and move on?

What if there's nothing there when we die? What if it goes black, then silent, then nothing? What if this is all there ever is. Is that okay? I had stopped believing in Jesus a long time before, and I had forgotten what had even betrayed that trust. Forgotten with a little help from decades of alcohol and delusion and the careful crafting of my own narrative. I had turned myself into a lie and forgotten all the reasons that made sadness run like tap water through my veins. I was always afraid to die, but I had nothing left to be excited for in life and at least death was something new.

Wish I could sing about anything other than death.

On the title track to Julien Baker's debut record, 2015's *Sprained Ankle*, she sings to her desire for finding something else in this world to think about beyond the end of it. It's a sparse and affecting record, written by Baker in her dorm room at Middle Tennessee State University before she recorded an EP with her friend Michael Hegner at the university studios Hegner had free time to utilize and then at Spacebomb Studios in Richmond, Virginia. Baker put the record on Bandcamp with a hand-drawn cover and low expectations, where it swiftly found an audience, then the attention of a record label—61631 Records—then the machine of the music industry.

I first heard about Baker while listening to podcasts in the apartment Alison and I shared above the garage downtown on Eighth Avenue. In 2015 Baker was a breath of unexpected fresh air. There has always been room in indie rock, folk music, and adjacent scenes for men to explore pain and suffering as this sort of nebulous idea of sadness and self-pity, but it was rare to hear someone so willing to open up in conversations regarding addiction, mental health, and a complicated relationship with personal faith. I heard Baker on a podcast talking openly about all of these things, the weight of the pain she carries with her, how it moves through her as she writes, and this lyrical catharsis and exploration of darkness not as a means of wallowing, but as a movement through cavernous darkness with hope of finding sources of light. It changed me.

When I hear "Sprained Ankle," even now, I hear the crunch of snow under my feet. I can feel the stark and abrupt cold of the winter in the Yukon on my face. I am bundled as warmly as I can be, walking down a street I know in everything but name, going nowhere to achieve nothing but will tell myself this is all part of a life. Small journeys to nowhere until there are no more journeys left to make. Baker's guitar is gentle, chords are careful and sharp, each one an accent on a point that is yet to be made.

Isn't this weather nice, are you okay?

You can get used to sadness; it can become a part of you. Not like a limb or an affectation but like a presence, a smell you can't place and are unsure if anyone else is aware of. I thought a lot about sadness and I thought a lot about death, and for a long time these two parallel lines threatened to intersect. That they never did is not a miracle or a virtuous triumph. There is something in Baker's work that I felt deep inside of the parts of my soul yearning for someone to hear them, the addiction and the doubt and the wavering faith. The despair not as sadness but lamenting and processing. It's easy to get used to sad, and it's easy to write sad off as wholly unproductive. But sadness can be the building block for endless scores of healing if you take time to walk away with lessons from all the times it cuts you.

Describing music as sad is a disservice to the impact emotional devastation has on our lives. When we describe joy there opens an array of emotions and adjectives, because we expect joy to be an onslaught of earthly delights. Sad becomes a concept spoken with a hushed voice or a somber tone. But sadness, true sadness done and told just right, is a world of possibility. This might be the true hidden promise of dad rock. There is sadness in here; there is something dark and somber, words hardened by distant memories and regret that are coupled together with strings and keys to create something truly beautiful. There is nothing more beautiful than surviving, emerging through hardship to share and mark on the path where you stood and where you stumbled, so that someone coming behind you might see all the places you faltered with the hope that they might avoid your fate, or if they don't at least they know they're not the only one who knows how it feels to fall.

Julien Baker has spent a career crafting words around the truth hidden in the fall. That she is here to sing and tell these stories is a testament to how deep the blade can go while still leaving you with blood to spare. The first time I heard Baker talk about her work on a music podcast I can no longer remember the name of, she talked about her faith, a wavering commitment to the idea of a tender relationship with a vengeful but delicate God, and something stirred in my heart about my own time spent whispering lost words to a God that might never hear me.

When I was very young, God was the promise of re-creation. He had, after all, made all this, and who is to say he couldn't remake it. Every night I asked that he find it within himself to make me whole, complete, the way I felt I was missing. That broken part desperate for someone to come along with enough glue and tape to mend the cracks and broken pieces into something resembling a life.

The promise of easy re-creation will always be more damaging than the truth, the reality that you can heal yourself only if you work hard to examine, process, move, and work through all the hard and broken parts of the soul and know that they might never repair. Some wounds never close, continuing to bleed into all things, and it's only in becoming used to the blood that we learn to move on.

This is the promise of Baker's work. She is used to the blood, and it is a tender and mighty thing that she is able to do so much self-reflective work and maintain a grip on this world, become stronger for it. *Sprained Ankle* was a hit, an indie release that became a legend, the kind of story artists dream about. An EP with a hand-drawn cover becomes a life, becomes revelatory and unforgettable. A record that lives forever in people.

Baker toured, and she found people. Strangers messaged her on Instagram to tell her just how the words she sung had reached into some part of them that felt unheard for so long they wondered if they ever even had a voice.

In an interview in *Stereogum*, Baker talks about an interaction with a fan who was deeply moved by her song "Brittle Boned." After the show, he found her and told her, " 'I really needed to hear someone say that because I've been doing that. I've been killing parts of myself that I don't like, and it sucks to have to leave things behind and go through change, and it's hard.'" She answered, " 'Yeah, it's really hard, and you're a total stranger, but I'm so glad you're here.' That's what makes it worth it for me."

In the lede of the *Stereogum* piece, the writer, Gabriella Claymore, describes the album as the saddest album she has ever heard. *Sad* feels like it doesn't even begin to do the work to describe the emotional tasting platter that has begun to shift people's lives.

For a long time I felt sad, and because I felt sad I felt broken, and with all of these things I had started to give up. Nothing seemed to work. I had accepted Jesus and that left scars where it had promised to build me up. I had told myself secret truths of my own desires to be able to grow into my life as the woman I saw in my head and had been rejected for them. I had been beaten and thrown aside and told this was all going to be worth it. This would all build me to something. I lost lovers and friends to disease and addiction, and slipped ever deeper in the promise of the darkness at the bottom of the bottle. Nothing worked. It was all sadness, and I had long lost sight of what sadness was promising to fix if only I could stop destroying myself long enough to hear what it was saying.

Baker writes sad songs—this is a true and easy statement—but more than anything she creates the promise of what she has found on the other side of all difficult and terrifying things. *Sprained Ankle* is the promise of youth. She was just entering her twenties when it was released, and there are a lot of people who will look at someone's youth as a negative but never consider that someone can be so young and have already survived so much. The immense weight that is placed on young lives as they struggle to emerge into new decades and later years. Baker was surviving and shining a light back to show where she had gone for others to follow.

In October 2017 Baker released her follow-up record, *Turn Out the Lights*, and I thought that this was all over.

A friend of mine, who quit drinking two years before I did, refers to these sorts of things as trying to tip over a Coke machine. You never get it in one push; sometimes you have to rock it back and forth a few times before it finally goes over the edge. I have flirted with suicide my entire life. This is the intrusive thoughts, this is the mental illness and the divergency of my neuropathways. In my head I am always holding a gun to my temple, my finger ready to pull just one last time. I have tried to tip over so many Coke machines in my life. I came out as trans enough times that the words started to feel hollow and lifeless by the time they finally worked. I tried to quit drinking once or twice, but I had always found myself back there when I desperately needed to feel the embrace of nothing.

Baker's music is sad, but it challenges you to find some use for all this sadness, some purpose to all this pain. The promise of all these hollow ideas like addiction and religion is that there is some reason for all things. In 2017, with *Turn Out the Lights*, she added grand structure to the foundation built on her debut album: now her voice was presented in layers, guitars chiming in and out behind it. Her voice at times appears hushed, other times it is ethereal, and still other times it has a hint of anger. ANGER. Anger at how hard this has all been. That nothing is better, nothing is healed. Everything is breaking down, relationships are failing, and the more things become damaged the more it is easy to isolate yourself from people or feel anything real. It becomes impossible to imagine telling anyone how you feel or what you need.

On "Appointments," the lead single from *Turn Out the Lights*, Baker works through this as I sit alone in my apartment and think about death. She is in a losing battle in a relationship; she is feeling like she has become someone that might never get better. Maybe she will always continue to be this bad. Maybe we are all pieces of an anxious and depressed machine that is nonetheless capable of something real. What if we fight for that—what if we stop ignoring the parts of us we tell ourselves are bad?

I told my partner I was trans because I was tired and because I thought she would hate me for it, and among the reasons she would come to hate me in time, being trans was never one of them. She hated me for the mistakes I made, the ways in which I lied and hurt her and the way I refused to take responsibility for the ways I hurt people, even when they hurt me as well. We are none of us blameless in the destruction we visit upon the people in our lives; there is no psychic damage we have suffered that makes the pain we continue to inflict on others worthwhile. It's only that sometimes we tell ourselves that we are damaged and sad and this is all we are owed in this world.

I left the partner who helped me come out as trans for someone else, eternally chasing the idea that there was another person out there who could make me feel whole and real somehow. Desperate for someone to be the reason why I became better instead of knowing that it would take working on myself to hold on to that feeling for good. When I told my ex that I had cheated on her and that I was leaving her for someone else, she destroyed my house in righteous fury, smashed my kitchen table on my foot and broke my toe. I told myself I deserved it too. Sometimes my toe pops out of joint still, and I still think I deserved it.

I chased all my needs and feelings into a new relationship like gasoline chasing a box of matches, and for a while the heat felt good. It felt good until it burned all the way through and left nothing behind but ash and memories and everything was failing. All of these things had promised to fix me and they were all failing. God and alcohol and transitioning were all supposed to FIX me. And here nothing had. Paranoia returned, anxiety heightened, and depression became worse than ever. In the back of my mind I began to plan leaving the Yukon for good.

In November 2017, my partner and I got into an argument on the phone; the distance between us was all that remained now that the needle had moved beyond empty. It was late at night and I needed to go for a walk, to feel the air on my face again. Black jeans, black hoodie, black leather jacket. Black hair. Black night. I walked out onto Eighth Avenue, where I had lived in three different apartments. Where the streets are not paved at all. The white tether of headphones from my phone to my ears was the only color against the darkness surrounding me, and for a while I could just hear music.

For a while I could just hear music, then I heard someone call me a faggot, then there was a fist in my right eye socket, then I was spinning and there was another voice yelling into the night saying "What the fuck is happening" and then there were footsteps running away and I was on the ground. I scurried back home. I called the cops and told them I was jumped outside my apartment. They asked me who it was and I described the memory of a man. The dispatcher laughed at me when I told her maybe it's because I'm trans, that I had been out publicly now for just a few weeks, maybe a month. She asked me what I wanted the cops to do, arrest every man in town because of one punch?

I drank.

The next day my landlord, the man who used to be my boss for the few months I worked as a locksmith and had long been someone I considered a friend, told me that he had a feeling he knew who jumped me. He said I likely knew them too. Told me maybe I shouldn't tell everyone about all the details of my life and things like this wouldn't happen. Friendly threats dressed up as advice.

I drank.

I was wrapping up a job installing doors at an assisted living facility in a new part of the city that was being constructed to meet the demand of Whitehorse's growing populace, and someone left a note on the window of my 1995 Nissan Pathfinder that threatened to kill me. I probably knew him too.

I drank.

I decided to leave, to move to Toronto. Everyone knew me here, and I no longer believed I knew myself. All I'd done here is drink, party, work, fuck, drink, black out, walk home angry, drink. I had become a void. No one wanted to hire a trans door repair person anymore anyway. I made plans; I broke them. I packed all my belongings and gave things away, put boxes into my parents' basement and left my cat Charlie with them too. I wondered if we would ever see each other again, and I cried at this, and it was the first time I had processed something that felt sad and real at the same time in what felt like forever. And then I was on a plane, and then I was gone.

I'll believe you if you make me feel something.

I always wanted home to fix something. To provide the answer and to tell me who I was. I wanted to be the person everyone expected because then your course is charted, requires no work or planning. But you will never make it through this world on autopilot.

Baker's finest work is her 2021 album *Little Oblivions*. With every year behind her she allows herself just that much more grace in self-reflection. There is rarely a songwriter as honest as she is, sharing careful, tender, and angry words about the ways she is struggling to make it through. There has been great success in her life, not just with her two critically acclaimed solo records but the EP she made with Phoebe Bridgers and Lucy Dacus under the name boygenius. And we like to imagine that you become successful enough to outrun the demons of your heart and mind, but that's never really quite true.

Wish that I drank because of you
And not only because of me.

In the essay that accompanies *Little Oblivions*, writer Hanif Abdurraqib captures the truth and beauty of Baker's work: "The grand project of Julien Baker, as I have always projected it onto myself, is the central question of what someone does with the many calamities of a life they didn't ask for, but want to make the most out of."

There is something to be said for choosing to live, and no longer hiding the parts of you that you feel make you seem broken or unworthy. How do we examine ourselves and our souls and still find the value in our hearts? We ask ourselves this without knowing, without always finding the words. But Baker does.

In 2021, when *Little Oblivions* was released, I got sober. I had been out for long enough that my name had changed for the third time to one that felt like mine. I had love in my life and so many things I always dreamed of. And still I had darkness. I still feel sad and I still feel damaged and I still struggle with the pull of the void that once felt like all I had.

I never felt like I deserved any of this. On "Song in E," Baker wonders the same, looking for someone to cast her out for all the cracks in the porcelain. God and the world that claims him create this idea of evil, and that idea of evil festers in us, creates value, creates shame. She opens painfully, wishing that she drank for any reason other than her own needs and desires, desperately searching for an enemy that isn't her in all of this pain. Eager for the anger and ire that will follow her drunken parade of worst thoughts.

Give me no sympathy.

Baker can craft so much out of so little, a piano played softly in a room that you can imagine empty and hushed, watching her choose each new chord with careful vision. "Song in E" is devastating as it sings to the heart of the addict who craves not just the substance but the judgment for its presence in our life.

It's the mercy I can't take.

She is stunned, like so many of us have been, to find mercy where she can only imagine judgment, as we have been told we deserve or have earned for our sins and our flaws. We may want to be cast aside for all the things we have done so we can wither away alone. But that isn't real, and that isn't how we grow or move on. We can only do that if, despite all our dark and sad places, we understand that we deserve love and the breadth of this world, and that is the hardest promise to accept.

We're all supposed to try

"FAREWELL TRANSMISSION"
SONGS: OHIA

I landed in Toronto late at night in January in the middle of a bitter snowstorm. I thought I had left the cold and the darkness behind me in the Yukon, yet here it was waiting to greet me. As if the worst parts of home had arrived ahead of time to remind me I would never be free of them.

I had friends, Paul and Amy, who had seen my desperate Instagram stories looking for a bed to sleep in and offered me a place to stay while I looked to find a new name for home. Paul met me at the train station, my hard-shell luggage weighed down with the life I fled carelessly stuffed away. The snow had fallen so heavy and thick that we had to struggle just to drag my aging dollar store luggage up the sidewalk. Sweating as the snow and the damp cold air hit my face. I had grown up in winter, I come from cold, but this felt different, air that was less crisp and clean than I was used to, not as cold but heavier. Denser. Different. I felt a slight thrill knowing that cold could feel different from how I've ever known it.

We made our way through the snow, my luggage wheels making lines in the snow showing where we had been. Fresh fallen snow leaving a clean canvas for the journey forward. I didn't know the directions home for the first time in my life, everything in the city dark and hazy, lit only by yellowed street lights, the whispers of white and red from passing headlights, and open signs left on in shop windows despite the doors being closed and locked.

We got home, dragged our half-lifeless bodies into the loft, left my suitcases to rest at the foot of the bed in the perfect sanctuary of a spare bedroom. We passed beers around a table and drank triumphantly to our arduous journey here as a record spun softly in the background. Braving the outdoors only to stand out on the small landing at the top of a fire escape and smoke cigarettes in the cold and stare into a gray-black sky hiding behind snow that continued to fall.

Suddenly everything felt new.

In my last days before leaving Whitehorse, I made a mixtape for the stereo in my '95 Nissan Pathfinder, a tape to listen to as I said goodbye to all things. I pulled favorites from the IKEA shelves in my apartment as I gathered records into boxes to store in my parents' basement. Hours of time I had set aside for packing, cleaning, and saying goodbye were spent instead lying on the floor of my living room with a bottle of mid-tier scotch and a notepad, scribbling a track list and a vision for the future.

I rarely made tapes with a plan, as I rarely approached anything in life with one, but I always like to think how it's all going to end and with the tape it was always going to be "Farewell Transmission."

Real truth about it is, no one gets it right.

"Farewell Transmission" is the lead track from the somewhat confusingly named *Magnolia Electric Co.* (the band changed names to Magnolia Electric Co. around the same time), a record from the band Songs: Ohia and the album that serves as a transition from one band name to another on the road map of Jason Molina's career. Molina's music was the through line connecting names, strands of roots, Americana and folk, country to a point, rock and roll to a fault. I've always loved a singer with cracks you can hear, like paper worn thin by time that shudders every time the wind brushes against it. A voice that reminds you of where it's been, that isn't afraid to be earnest and to yearn for something, or to be afraid of what might be coming.

I left home partially because I was afraid. Afraid of the reaction to my coming out, afraid of the people who reacted with derision or violence. The first few days after my arrival in Toronto, the snow was so heavy and ever falling that the only option we had was to stay inside. We made coffee, Paul made oatmeal with blueberries in the morning, and we sat in the warmth of home and safety. I was glad for the snow, glad for the cold. It was familiar enough but different, and it kept us inside unless we left to stand outside and smoke or breathe new air for a minute or two and I was still afraid.

It's a cliché to put "Farewell Transmission" at the end of the mixtape I made for my '95 Nissan to listen to as I drove around saying goodbye to all the people I assumed I would never see again. Cliché to have it wrap up as I drove to the dump to throw out boxes of things that used to belong to someone who used to look like the memory of me. But I was at the end of all I could see, and clichés were what remained.

Jason Molina died on March 16, 2013, of massive organ failure after a decade of alcoholism slowly ate away at him. I remember first seeing the news on Facebook, where posts started to appear with a link to a YouTube video of the song, with lyrics perfectly placed in memorial,

I will be gone, but not forever.

"Farewell Transmission" was released in 2003, a decade before Molina's death at thirty-nine. Former bandmates, friends, and family say that his relationship to drinking had turned into something darker over the last decade of his life, starting around the same time that "Farewell Transmission" opened the shift of the band's name from Songs: Ohia to Magnolia Electric Co. In a Tumblr post prefacing an old tour diary, longtime Molina bandmate Jason Groth writes, "It was clear to me starting as early as 2003 that he and the bottle had a complicated relationship. It wasn't until 2009, and really later than that, that the truth about how bad that relationship had gotten really came to light."

We're all supposed to try.

I didn't visibly have a problem with alcohol. This is what I told myself when I lived in the Yukon, where I never left the house without a flask of bourbon somewhere on me. I once drank a bottle of scotch at home, a flask on the walk to, and an assortment of beers at a house party I don't remember being at. I blacked out more frequently, sometimes being aware of having been at a party at all only once I was tagged in a photo on Facebook. Sometimes I listened to stories told around hangover breakfast tables to recollect my own actions through the night so I could claim I recalled more than I did. I hid who I was—blackout drinker, trans, queer—with ease. I had been hiding so many things for so long, it was hard to know what was the closet and what was visible in the light.

"Farewell Transmission" pops up every year on the anniversary of Molina's death, because it's easy to imagine it as a song saying goodbye. Molina died of complications from his long battle with an addiction to alcohol and in death became a songwriter writing eternal farewells to himself and all people. His demise read between every line by those looking for clues as to how his life ended the way it had. I can appreciate the desire to find answers this way: How could a man who worked so hard and created so much beautiful and profound work leave this earth the way he did? It's harder, maybe, to accept that there are more difficult forces at play on the periphery of this. That he couldn't afford the healthcare he needed to survive. In the last few years of his life he had taken to asking for material support from fans to keep himself afloat, and even that wasn't enough to save him. Relying on the kindness of community and strangers to keep him alive.

Long dark blues.

Paul and Amy were kind enough to let me stay with them longer than any of us had planned. We ate breakfasts together, had coffee, smoked cigarettes on the landing, and listened to records. I drank, but it always felt forced. Read a dog-eared copy of Imogen Binnie's *Nevada*. I could tell when it was time to leave the Yukon, and I could tell when it was time to leave the temporary sanctuary I had found living among old moving boxes in a spare room granted to me by the kindness of community. They asked if I had any luck finding an apartment enough times that I knew I had to find one before this all fell apart.

Listen.

A friend had a spare room in her apartment, affordable enough and ready enough to let me move in. I gathered a life into luggage once more and moved myself into a room I could unpack in and claim as a home. I set up a life with a bed and a roof over my head. Smoked cigarettes under a tree in the front of our building. Watched cars drive by, said hello to strangers as they walked out to meet the day.

Shortly after I moved in we had a party, a housewarming for me and a birthday for my roommate. Friends moved in and out of the building as the night shifted into darkness. I made drinks; we drank beers out front while we smoked and laughed. A perfect evening. The next morning, I laid flat on my bed as my roommate came in to agree the party was perfect and my response was that it was, and that I really wanted to die.

I had run from home afraid of something lurking in the darkness, and it took being away from the streets that plagued me to see that what I had been most afraid of was the danger I posed to myself. I had been trying to take a life that hadn't been working and make it fit into new surroundings, and never once did I consider that this was an opportunity to start living with new foundations under tired feet.

On March 24, 2019, I quit drinking.

I don't think of Jason Molina as sad, although his work is often melancholic and dark and sad a little. *Sad* as a singular word feels too easy, like cheating on the test of a man's life. He feels like a man who was swimming against the tide for longer than he was moving with it, but desperate to keep going. He approached songwriting the way my dad worked, the way he had taught me how to approach my own: all work is labor, and labor requires time and effort. In a 2006 interview for the *Chicago Tribune*, Molina told Jessica Hopper, "I write about eight hours a day, and I throw away most of what I write."

There's a familiarity in Molina, often photographed in a Carhartt hat or clad in workwear. He was raised in northern Ohio, in an industrial town in the early '70s, by his father, a middle school teacher, in a single-wide mobile home. His mother was an alcoholic, staying home in the daytime to try and manage her addiction. She got sober on Molina's graduation day, but the threat of addiction lingered in Molina's mind.

It's unfair that musicians who struggled with their addictions become branded as sad and lonesome writers when they die. Elliott Smith, Nick Drake, Townes Van Zandt, and Jason Molina. This is something that happens predominantly to men, and maybe it's just that men are prone to this kind of destructive sadness and maybe it's just a sinister coincidence that they could never get the help they needed to live with their own saddest parts. In their absence, every tender word they found to describe the darkness of their world turns from poetic beauty to anguished revelation.

The day I quit drinking, I walked downtown to get a tattoo at a queer clothing store on Queen Street in Toronto with a tattoo shop set up in the back room. I smoked half a pack of cigarettes on the walk down in an effort to burn away the lingering threats of my own intrusive thoughts that remained buoyant in the previous night's alcohol. I wanted this to be the last time I drank, to be the last time I felt this weight. I played Dwight Yoakam on my phone and thought about my mom, thought about the music in my parents' house and my mom telling me the story of how my dad quit drinking just by declaring he was done with it.

It's easy to want Molina's music to only be sad now that he's gone. His absence and his loss are sad, and the truth of the final decade of his life is that of a man slowly losing a fight he was desperate to win. "Farewell Transmission" is so often used in eulogy, and maybe in that eulogy there is an urge to choose something beyond hopelessness or defeat. "Farewell Transmission" is sad only in passing glance. This is a man determined to try, even when the battle he was bound to lose started to linger in his brain.

I will try, and know whatever I will try.

I thought about what it means to choose to live, and what it would mean to lose yourself to the worst impulses of addictive tendencies. I thought around my intrusive thoughts urging me to walk into traffic. I chose to stay on the sidewalk. I walked into the tattoo shop, another trans woman gave me a tattoo of a harpy on my right arm, and each burning line from the needle felt like pain I wanted to remember and relive forever. This is how it feels to choose to live.

I wanna see it when you find out what comets, stars, and moons are all about

"CAR"

BUILT TO SPILL

I've made mixtapes for a lot of people over the years. A compulsion that started when I was young, holding my fingers tight to the record and play buttons on a shitty plastic boombox tuned loosely to the only good radio station in Whitehorse so I could put "Everything's Zen" by Bush on a tape. As I got older I made them for friends, potential lovers, long drives. I bought cars with tape decks just to have an excuse to make another tape, one that I could play when I would drive out onto the highway at night and be alone with my thoughts and meandering feelings. I learned to make tapes from my dad and my memories of his abandoned habits, but I don't remember what was on any that I made. Their track lists are just loose recollections, fragments of songs that bleed into each other, like the time I knew I needed to get "Everything's Zen" to put right after "Connection" by Elastica.

Friends had tapes that lived in their cars, each one a soundtrack to a life. No two the same, but all of them made with love and intention. I'm not sure this is how it works for everyone, but these songs all function as the card catalogue to a life. Choose one, and it will show you where to go to remember all the things you thought were missing.

I turned songs into sequences on mixtapes for long enough that I can still hear the transitions at the end of tracks, connections that once lived on tapes I don't fully remember. Sometimes the memory is better than the truth anyway. I made tapes to explain myself, a formerly quiet and shy introvert able to communicate only through songs strung together in perfect sequence committed to tape or burned into a CD-R.

The first time I ever heard Built to Spill, it was on a mixtape a friend made me after I said I thought Dinosaur Jr. was a better band than Nirvana. We had stayed up late, long after the bar closed, drinking stolen wine and smoking borrowed cigarettes. I was doing my best to seem just interesting and challenging enough to be worth listening to. I didn't know who I really was, the skeleton of me buried under the well-crafted pretension of a young adulthood spent hiding my true feelings away. I let music tell the story I wanted people to believe. The morning after, I was given a gift: a tape called *Dinosaur Jr. is not better than Nirvana*. The first song on it was "Carry the Zero" by Built to Spill.

I met Lysh for the first time at a music festival, but she doesn't remember the moment. It was 3:00 a.m., maybe 4:00. Her band Sheezer, an all-female Weezer cover band, had just finished playing a show at a bar called the Ship in St. John's, Newfoundland, at a festival our friends had just started. I had shown up to the venue late, well after the show had ended, and Lysh was used to weird, annoying guys hanging around shows long after they had ended. At the time, it was easy to perceive me as just one more annoying guy. And she had little patience for one more. I had a crush on Lysh right away, standing triumphant and exhausted all at once in line with the other members of Sheezer.

The second time Lysh and I met, it was backstage at the Dawson City Music Festival in the Yukon. She was there playing with long-running Canadian indie rock band By Divine Right, and I was once more perceived as just some guy hanging out. I had friends playing the festival, and for a short few years I ran a small record label out of my apartment called Headless Owl Records, and so I was there for "business reasons" that were never fully fleshed out. Convenient covers for the truth that I just liked to hang out backstage, a place where I could hide. Lysh had seen and met a hundred people exactly like the version of me I presented, and once again we failed to cross the boundary from friend of friend to anything more.

Built to Spill existed like ghosts to me, appearing out of nowhere on mix CDs made by friends or as references in music magazines. Every time a song appeared, the stray thought entered my mind that I should know more about this band, so aligned with the music that I love and in conversation with the songs that I had loved and built into mixtapes and memories. The lo-fi pop fuzz of it all elicited an instant pleasure response.

But sometimes I would just forget things unless I wrote them down, and it took a while for Built to Spill to stick with me. I wish I could have been cool when I was young, I wish I could claim I bought *There's Nothing Wrong with Love* in 1994, but I just wasn't. I was too busy hiding my life away.

Sometimes we just have to wait, not for serendipity per se but for the right time, to be ready. I wasn't ready for Built to Spill the first time I heard them on a mixtape, but every time it started with "Carry the Zero," which bled into "Supernova" by Liz Phair on side A of *Dinosaur Jr. is not better than Nirvana*, I flirted with being ready a little more.

Lysh and I eventually became friends; she followed me back on Instagram in 2015, and I remember thinking this was a big move forward. We made small talk in comments over the years, never growing too close but cementing a friendship.

We started to talk a lot in 2017, when our lives began imploding in parallel. She had moved to Vancouver for a relationship that wasn't working, and I was in a vacuum of panic waiting for my chance to run and leave home behind. Suddenly we were sending supportive DMs, then texting. Talking about music we loved, the outside world closing in on our tender hearts. Lysh and I share a deep love of Sleater-Kinney, and we bonded over favorite songs and best memories. She told me about her collection of mixtapes, and I fell in love forever.

When I fled to Toronto in the middle of a dark and cold January, she was the first person I texted once I had safely arrived at my new temporary sanctuary. We bonded over our persistent feelings of solitude and isolation, watched old episodes of *Chopped* together by syncing pause and play at just the right time on less-reputable streaming sites, and bet on who we thought would win it all.

When I moved into the spare room of a friend's house—one of Lysh's former bandmates in Sheezer—I talked about her endlessly but was unsure of where my feelings might take us. We started a podcast about Sleater-Kinney just to have an excuse to talk, and we made plans to hang out if she ever returned to Toronto. I asked my roommate if she knew anything I didn't. I felt like I was sixteen; I felt alive. There was a thrill in not knowing, and suddenly the future became something I could never predict.

I don't know what's on every mixtape I've ever made, but Lysh does. She has binders of track lists from all the tapes she has made over the years, carefully catalogued to ensure she never made the same tape twice. There's a life you can trace through the sequences she has carefully outlined, recollections of people and places and times she can recall. Music building behind the story she wants to tell.

I quit drinking a few months before Lysh and I saw each other for the first time in years. Partially because I knew I needed to do it, and partially because I wanted to do it in support of her desires to do the same. Without booze to kill the day, I sank into my secondary addictions, caffeine and cigarettes. Made playlists for my daily walk down the street to my favorite coffee shop, Empire Espresso (RIP), where I would sit on the bench out front with its fading blue paint, smoke cigarettes, and listen to music or make idle chatter with regulars and new neighbors. I felt like I was part of the movement of the city that had once been so unfamiliar to me.

I listened to "Car" every day on my walk.

"Car" is the standout track from the Built to Spill record I was not cool enough to know about when it was released in 1994, *There's Nothing Wrong with Love*. Produced by future indie superstar producer Phil Elk, Built to Spill emerged from Boise, Idaho, in the post-Nirvana scramble of the mid-'90s, as labels and audiences turned to look for what might come next. Doug Martsch, front man and principal songwriter for the band, had spent some time in the band Treepeople, an alt-rock band built of Boise band members formed in Seattle who played music shaded in colors of Twin/Tone bands like Hüsker Dü and the Replacements, Dinosaur Jr. and the thrashier impulses of Sonic Youth. When eager eyes looked to the frontier for new arrivals, Martsch was there already, known to the scene, waiting for the right moment to be heard once more.

There's Nothing Wrong with Love is the second record from Built to Spill, and the first to cause a commotion in their name. More experimental maybe than Treepeople, softer in parts and louder in others, but tender in place of what had once felt more abrasive. It's an album of love songs, and an album of cautious optimism and careful movements into growing older. Looking back and forward in fluid motions, wistful for what has come and what has gone, and grateful for the road ahead.

The first mix I ever made for Lysh I labored over for days. I didn't know what all was going to be on it; I just knew it had to be perfect. It had to say all the things I needed it to, to tell the story I was eager for her to hear, and it started with "Car."

I need a car, you need a guide, who needs a map?

Lysh and I started dating the week she came to Toronto for a visit and a recording session. We went out for nachos, went to see a friend's band play, went back for nachos again, stayed up and walked the streets of Toronto together at night, newly sober, isolated together. Smoking cigarettes to burn anxious feelings off at my fingertips. That night I told her I had a problem, that I had a crush on her and I couldn't shake it, that I was afraid of a thousand things but most of all losing her in my life, but that I was learning to not be afraid of life or consequences anymore and I was finding so many things to look down the road for. It was the first night we spent together.

I wanna see movies of my dreams.

"Car" is a slow and careful song in contrast to the movement it implies: cars that deliver us swiftly to destinations and the end of a journey. Martsch sings in his wavering tenor through the desire to experience the world through someone else, or maybe with them.

You get the car, I'll get the night

And then a small pause, a breath,

Off.

"Car" grows over time, gentle and slow at first but building in intensity over time, gathering itself in preparation for a grand statement. The desire to grow and change and never be the same but to always be here to feel something, even when it's hard. I had run from a thousand lives and been afraid and angry and tired and mad for so long, and here I was all those things still but something more. Something beyond the boundaries of a life I thought I knew. Something real, often broken or tired but real.

If I don't die or worse, I'm gonna need a nap.

I told Lysh I loved her after we had been dating for three days, and it was only a few months before she moved back to Toronto, sharing the spare room of a friend's apartment for a month before we moved into our first apartment together. A month later we got a dog, then on her birthday a cat. We built a life together slowly, steadily. We found a future to build together, marked days and time with our memories together. Went on drives and listened to playlists and on every one I snuck "Car" in somewhere, a reminder of where we had been, all the places we might go together, and all the movements of a life we might discover with each other.

I never thought about love when I thought about home

"BLOODBUZZ OHIO"
THE NATIONAL

I am following my own steps right now, up the street, my street, with my dog, Bowie, ahead of me and only sometimes at my heels when he stops to sniff at the ground and the grass and all the things he knows will always be there.

This is our route, the same steps following a similar path every night. The same left turn, the same right. The same crosswalks and the same overflowing garbage cans wafting the perfume of their persistent filth into the air.

We're on the street next to the apartment where I live with Lysh and our two cats—one with cancer (Nina), one without (Ramona)—and Bowie, our German shepherd/corgi rescue dog. Every night when we walk outside, we pass by the silent sentinel of our rusted and graying 2008 Dodge Grand Caravan, standing stoic and silent and forlorn in the parking lot. It hasn't moved from this spot in weeks, or maybe months. It has a dead transmission, but it is alive with the spirit of many fond memories that we cannot bring ourselves to part with, and so it just stands there. Waits to be given the opportunity to live.

I tried to move to Toronto for the first time in 2016. An attempt that just did not take, a passive attempt, waiting to see what would happen if I left my small town in the Yukon for the biggest city in Canada. Maybe the shocking contrast between Whitehorse and Toronto would be a jolt to my system, a lightning strike to my long dead heart and soul, and I would reanimate as someone new, someone perfect. I had a dead transmission, and I was also just waiting to be fixed so I could shift gears, live again.

I love to talk about trying while doing nothing, and I am all too intimate with the silhouette of failure. When I lived here ever so briefly in 2016, a year before I came out as trans, I thought this city would somehow flip a switch within me and I would cease to be a man and be reborn as who I wanted to be. I was an adult who believed in the promise of magic. The sanctuary of naivete.

At night in 2016, alone and empty, I would stalk the streets of my neighborhood alone, with no dog to guide or slow my steps. I would wander the city and listen to the National in my headphones and think about how I was supposed to live in a city, a city that felt like the backdrop in a song, but I somehow wasn't sticking to the background of this urban diorama. I would walk down under the bright lights of an endless city, try and catch my reflection in windows as I passed by, but all I ever saw was a strange man staring back at me and no switch ever got flipped.

I would hear the silken baritone of the National vocalist Matt Berninger enter my thoughts through headphones connected by their tenuous tether to my rose gold iPhone 6, and I would see myself in all the reflective surfaces as filtered through this man singing tender and emotionally destructive songs about alcohol and despair, and I would tell myself that maybe this is all that I am, all that I am supposed to be. I would walk home alone, sit out on the steps in the sticky heat of a Toronto summer, drink brown liquor out of a rocks glass until I felt nothing, and fall asleep in my dark bedroom apartment and hope to never wake up.

I always did, and I never thought to ask myself what I could be doing differently.

Now, out here in the night with my dog after a long day, there is a moment of clear understanding that flows in and fills all the crevices of my mind and spirit, out here when the sky is settled and dark like a blanket pulled over our eyes, with the birds gathered to sing the B-sides and offcuts of their songbooks.

The night is where I let my mind gather all the items it has strewn about. Sometimes working through all the events of the past or of the day, but more often of the series of days that have turned into weeks, into months, into years. A long thread that weaves throughout memories and black holes and hurdles. The night is when I think about home, not the one where I will return to lay my head but the one that raised me. The home that I left, the home that ultimately rejected me when it saw me for the first time.

My hand reaches into my pocket, finds a lighter without a half-full pack of cigarettes to marry it to. I am trying to quit, I think to myself as I try to not also think about how I would rather not quit. Sometimes I'm not quitting at all; sometimes I tell myself it's okay because the day has been hard, and my heart hurts the right way, and I am allowed this one simple dalliance. I haven't drunk alcohol in over three years and haven't I earned this? Have my lips not earned the promise of its flame?

This is all a distraction, my brain sending out impulses to keep my thoughts frayed and scattered. An entire day spent taking in information that I have to somehow find the means to expunge, to burn it all away. I used to pour myself a glass of bourbon, mix a careful cocktail over the perfect ice cube, and then finish the bottle clean, lying in a bathtub for an hour with an empty box of pizza dead on the floor next to me. But I don't, I can't, do that anymore, and there's nothing sober in this world that replaces the sensation of fading away.

I find my phone instead and pull it out to find a song to drive into my ears and distract my brain from thinking about all the habits I am quitting and the way my heart hurts or my brain feels like screaming into the night sky in hopes that God themself might hear and return an answer. AirPods and noise cancelling and Bluetooth 3.0 working in unison to protect all that I am.

You know, the first time I heard the National I thought they were British.

There was something tonally in there, in Matt Berninger's baritone or the way every minor key felt like the rain falling around you on a dark and cloud-covered evening, feet falling hard and flat on wet cobblestones on a busy West London street. I have never spent enough time in London to know the feel of its streets myself, but in my head when I listen to them it creates an image that feels real all the same. It turns out they're not British, they're just dour but from Ohio.

The National is, more specifically, from Cincinnati, despite widely being considered a Brooklyn band. While in college in Cincinnati, singer Matt Berninger started his first band, called Nancy in tribute to his mom, with future the National bass player Scott Devendorf and other friends of theirs attending the University of Cincinnati. They wanted, like so many college rock bands and so many men, to be like Pavement.

Every now and then I remember being on a blind date with a woman who was well and truly drunk before I ever sat with a false bravado down into our squeaky corner booth, one with terrible lighting and worse acoustics, and her taking swift stock of all I was pretending to be in an instant. With a grandiose wine glass gesture in my direction, she said that I looked like one of those guys that's really into Pavement. There is nothing more damning than being so thoroughly seen so quickly.

I was really into Pavement, and in my desperate grasps at a life of doomed masculinity, I was also trying to pull off an effortless Matt Berninger from the National vibe. None of this ever took, a slick veneer that slowly peeled and fell away.

THE NATIONAL BECAME A BROOKLYN BAND when the various members—brothers Aaron and Bryce Dessner, brothers Scott and Bryan Devendorf, and Matt Berninger, brotherless in the band but not in life—found themselves leaving college and

Cincinnati behind to find new lives for themselves as postcollegiate adults in Brooklyn. Leaving your home behind to find new opportunities in a city where no one knows your name or recalls all of your imagined slights and failings is a feeling all too familiar to me. Sometimes homes remember too much. Their first record is a strange artifact to revisit in the rearview. A self-titled album released in 2001 that felt like a grasp at an alt-country Americana that was taking up valuable space in music magazines as the next great thing, buoyed by the crossover success of albums like Wilco's landmark *Yankee Hotel Foxtrot* and ex Whiskeytown front man Ryan Adams's *Heartbreaker* and follow-up *Gold*. Songs like "American Mary" and "Cold Girl Fever" are hints at what the band would go on to become with subsequent releases, but it feels muted and tame in contrast to the boldness of their modern era.

The follow-up, *Sad Songs for Dirty Lovers*, released in 2003, has a more robust flavor but is no less starkly different from their modern work. They were after all still finding their footing in a musical landscape that was rapidly changing below them, as the 2000s shifted away from the popularity of Americana in favor of indie rock and up-tempo songs that you could do cocaine to. It was only when they signed to Beggars Banquet and released *Alligator* in 2005 and then *Boxer* in 2007 that the band found the success that would make them into grander visions of themselves. Transform them from five men making music together into a machine that was always on a stage in a city somewhere pretending to be fully complete versions of themselves, men that looked like they listened to Pavement performing to crowds of people who looked like they listened to the National.

At home in the Yukon, I would occasionally run into the woman who said I looked like a guy that was really into Pavement, and while we never spoke much after our one-and-done attempt at a life together, I always wondered if she could see through me, or if I was only ever being read as a shell. A walking shiny veneer that was really into Pavement.

Home is a looming presence on the National's fifth record, 2010's *High Violet*. The band was exhausted by the success they had found with their previous albums. *Boxer* and *Alligator* had become critical and commercial successes and had taken the band from Americana curiosity to touring indie rock juggernaut. *Alligator* had been on numerous end-of-year best lists and was *Uncut Magazine*'s second-best album of the year in 2005. *Boxer*, with exponential growth behind it, was on a parade of lists for the best songs and album that year.

They had played their first late-night TV spot, performing "Fake Empire" on *The Late Show with David Letterman* in July 2007, and had crossed the threshold from rising star to a supernova gathering heat. They had quit their jobs by this point (singer Matt Berninger had for a time worked in advertising) and were now something new, reborn in the light of a new city. Full-time musicians who used to be something different, something that dreamed to be where they found themselves now.

With critical success, their lives had slowly turned into a road show; the eternal ballet of constantly moving from bus to stage to bus again and the endless repetition of a highway that never leads to home was taking its toll on the band, Brooklyn-based but not Brooklyn as a home. Ohio was no longer where they went to lay their heads when it was time to rest but was all the same where their roots had dug deep into the soil.

The street I am walking on now, in the dark with my dog and the nagging urge to smoke a cigarette, is in the west end of Toronto. I am not from here, but I am home all the same. I have learned in recent years to make peace with my home and happily tell people I'm from the Yukon. I tell anyone who asks the best way to get there is to go out to the street, turn left and then go up a way, and eventually you'll get there. Pause for laughter. Remembering it here on this street, my old home is just a series of dangerous firsts, where I drank for the first time, where I started smoking, where I got into fights, crashed cars, started a construction company, nearly died, lived and loved and fell apart. Memories of when it was my home, and now it is only where I am from.

After I moved back to the Yukon in 2016, having tried and failed to fit in on the streets of Toronto, I realized I was also not feeling at home in the Yukon anymore, and my brain started to nag at questions I thought I had buried. Old demons never rightfully exorcised getting louder, more urgent, unrelenting.

"Bloodbuzz Ohio," the lead single from 2010's *High Violet*, finds the National grappling with home, their hearts split between Brooklyn and Ohio with a divide that must have been made worse by time spent on the road. In an interview in *Uncut* magazine, guitarist Aaron Dessner said that they were in "a dark place. . . . It was exhaustion and everything that comes with being that fatigued, relationships were suffering. We almost broke up, actually." It was only in coming home and making a workspace that felt true to them, finding a new way to be the kind of band they were growing into, that they were able to make these songs work and to find a way forward.

TONIGHT, OUT HERE ON THE STREET, I am wearing clothes that aren't even clean. I am wearing leggings with a hole in the knee and a sports bra that is due for a wash. I have an oversized T-shirt, and my hair is messy enough to be noticed. What I'm wearing doesn't matter as I gather myself for a turn around the block. It's just the nighttime after all, and there is rarely anyone out here, other than the people who smoke on their front porches and who are always on a phone call, pausing every time I walk by and continuing when I'm just about out of earshot.

Stand up straight at the foot of your love
I lift my shirt up.

Berninger is in assessment of himself as a man in "Bloodbuzz Ohio," shedding his shirt like a snake would dead skin and laying bare what is fresh and raw underneath. Our clothes reveal ourselves, and they were once so important to the perception of who I was pretending to be. I looked like a man who loved Pavement because I wanted to look like the kind of man that Matt Berninger pretended to be in songs, and I thought maybe this would be the way I survived. I would certainly never leave the house to walk the dog without ensuring my costume was complete in case someone saw me. Always trying to give the appearance of being complete and whole and perfect, even when I was flawed.

In "Bloodbuzz Ohio," Berninger is singing to his home, his old home of Ohio that he doesn't live in anymore, the home he outgrew sometime in the past. "I still owe money . . . to the money I owe," he sings. "The floors are falling out from everybody I know," he continues, and I think about my own debt and my own friends back home who are there paying for homes and raising families and the tenuous nature of staying in a small town and becoming part of its system versus throwing all your money at escaping to find yourself somewhere new. I came here with nothing and continue to hold on to very little.

The bloodbuzz in the title is Berninger, fueled by alcohol, running the length of synapses to his brain to fire this memory of home. It is true that drinking can make you wistful and Berninger is known to be a fan of wine. He frequently performs with a bottle of it, and he sings often of his relationship to alcohol, and I think about how much I let alcohol as a personality overtake me. How I became enamored with expensive scotch and good whiskey and fine bourbon because those are extensions of a perception that a person can pretend is interesting very quickly. Some of the best addictions are born of a desire to create something real in ourselves.

Bowie stops to sniff at a lawn he sniffed this morning and every night and morning before this one because one time he found a slice of pizza there when I wasn't looking and managed to eat it all before I could stop him, and now he holds on to this beautifully misguided hope that the pizza he had once will return. That all good things come back and find us again.

I do not have the heart to tell him that truly good things never come back; the best we can do is hold on to their memories. We have to learn to become comfortable with loss. We continue our walk, and the streets are quiet and serene and devoid of anyone but us and the birds, except for the scant few on their front steps smoking their own cigarettes, and I often wonder if they're trying to quit like me or if they've just given up and accepted that sometimes we just like to hurt ourselves. Sometimes the only way we can feel something is to hurt ourselves.

Berninger sings, "I never thought about love when I thought about home," and I remember the bad date who said I looked like a Pavement fan, and all the other lost loves and failed romances and the dalliances and one-night stands, and how sometimes in a small town you end up dating someone because you woke up together after a party and decided to go for breakfast and then three weeks have gone by and you are still waking up together after parties. None of those were ever real, and few of them were ever love.

They aren't love like what I have right now, at home in the apartment we will return to when this walk is complete. When I am out here in my memories on this street, I think about home, but like Berninger I am not thinking about love. I am remembering the way my childhood home vibrates in the wintertime when the dam on the Yukon River isn't able to generate enough power for the city and the generator turns on. I think about the pictures on the wall in the living room of that home, my mom and dad sitting on the cliff just up the road from their house with their dogs Cassie and Molly, who passed away years ago but are fondly and eternally remembered.

For many years I tried to be a man like Berninger, but the more I listened to the National I realized that he felt everything so earnestly and vividly and real. Matt Berninger has stage fright, which is why he has a bottle of wine on stage; it helps relax him. You are only frightened when you are laying yourself bare, and I was never frightened to stand on a stage in front of people because they were never really seeing me. They were seeing the version of me I was pretending to be.

The National is the benchmark of a modern dad rock band. Over the years they have become fathers, but more than anything they have grappled with the emotional weight of aging and what it means to not be young and invincible anymore. What do we do with ourselves once we become brittle and vulnerable? Dad rock is so much less about being a father than it is about being a dad; it is about daring to be vulnerable and raw and the veracity with which you feel everything as so intense that only a singular vice will help quell the rising storm in your heart.

I never felt anything so real as the National did, and the more I became obsessed with them and the more I tried to pull off my best Matt Berninger impression as a personality, the more everything started to fall apart. I could never be him because I was not allowing myself to feel anything at all. And I had to let my guard down, stop pretending, stop closing all of my doors and windows and let the air in and my true emotions out for all to know. And once you start opening those doors, there is no turning back, and it is because of this that I was able to become the woman I had hidden away for so very long.

I think about all of this, and I hear the birds on a tree somewhere off in the distance from my home, my real home, here at the foot of this street I am walking on, and I think about all the terrible and beautiful things that lived in all the days before this one. I am only just now able to say that there is a fondness there for them.

When this song ends a new one will come forth. Eventually I switch off from the National and find something new and remember different days and recall old faces and cringe at different memories of mistakes, and I will feel all of it and crawl into bed with Lysh; our pets will climb onto the bed too. We will soberly lay ourselves to sleep, and I will wake up in the morning to do this exact walk all over again, and I am struck at how lucky I am to find myself here.

If the dead just go on living, well there's nothing left to fear

"ST. CLOUD"
WAXAHATCHEE

It's important to know how to end things. This is a lesson I learned in making mixtapes: you have to prepare for the end. Don't drag it out; leave a good memory right in the final minutes, before the tape runs out.

Katie Crutchfield always knew that "St. Cloud," the title track to her 2020 record, would come at the end. It's a sparse and beautiful album closer, opening with a recollection of her time in New York riding the M train before shifting its lens to St. Cloud, a small city in Florida where her father comes from. *St. Cloud* was her fifth record as Waxahatchee but the first to feature music rooted in the records of her youth, particularly Lucinda Williams. In an essay on her love of Williams's *Car Wheels on a Gravel Road* for *Stereogum* in 2018, she says, "I grew up in Alabama and in my early teens I was abruptly swept into punk. Country music was for my parents."

St. Cloud is Crutchfield learning to embrace home and change, and finding words to tell the stories of ghosts who had been following her. It's an autobiographical work that celebrates all the steps, good and painful, that helped her arrive at a safe distance from which to tell the truths she had been avoiding for too long, including getting sober in 2018 during Primavera Festival in Barcelona.

Album opener "Oxbow" champions the freshness of post-sobriety clarity, how it welcomes an opportunity to write new chapters for yourself. As with all self-reflective works, though, *St. Cloud* follows the peaks and valleys of an autobiographical journey through memories she cannot change or control, confronting the memories of lost loved ones and the painful recollections of the worst memories of herself that are all too common for people in recovery.

Where do you go when your mind starts
To lose its perfected shape?

What makes "St. Cloud" a perfect closer is the peace it finds in all these difficult memories, the challenges and issues faced in days past, cherishing the roots that grew into all this. In a track-by-track breakdown in *Pitchfork*, Crutchfield says of choosing the name for this song and naming the record after it, "I thought it would be a nice way to honor my dad."

I thought this would be a nice way to honor my dad too. The title for this book came to me well before the structure. It almost sounded funny at first, but the more I put it together the more I saw my dad in my memories of so many things and I wanted it to reflect how much my dad has meant to me. Thank you to my dad, Nick, for everything you taught me and for the guidance that got me here. Thank you for listening to the Waterboys in your headphones just loud enough that I could hear "Fisherman's Blues" escape the worn-thin foam covering your ears while you slept on the couch with a book folded face-down on your chest. Thank you for teaching me to push myself, and to never let failing stop me from trying.

Thank you to my mom, Linda, who listened to music on all the perfect days of my memories. Thank you for teaching me about telling stories with music as the backdrop, and for always supporting me regardless of how much it seemed like I might not succeed. My mom always told me she would be fine if I became a ditch digger as long as I was happy, and it took me a while, but I'm happy more than I'm not now. Like Katie Crutchfield, I was more into punk rock than country as a teen, but in adulthood and sobriety I've come to love the music that makes me think of home so much more.

St. Cloud was released in the early days of the COVID-19 pandemic in 2020, when Lysh and I had been living in our first apartment together for only a few months. At night I would take Bowie to the park and walk six feet away from everyone to be safe with *St. Cloud* in my headphones. The first song that made me cry was "St. Cloud," because it made me think of home, and it made me grateful for the one I had built here too. Thank you to Alysha, for your love, support, and guidance and for the home we've built together. Thank you for listening to me as I worked through the endless sections of this book, for reading it and hearing me read it time and again, and for your reminders that I used the wrong form of *its*.

Thank you as well to my sister, Corinna, who has always been there ahead of me, who introduced me to music and ideas that would live with me for a lifetime. Thank you for always being there to watch out for me, even and especially on the days I didn't know I needed someone to help.

Thank you to Jessica Hopper, without whom this book wouldn't have an end for me to arrive at. Thank you for your honest and careful guidance that helped me see what I was avoiding writing through. The hard stories and ghosts of the past. Thank you for all that you have done to build a foundation so many of us can stand on.

Thank you to Casey Kittrell for all of your work on this with me, for our conversations and your insightful edits, notes, and encouraging words. Thank you for helping ease my anxious mind as I challenged myself to be honest and vulnerable in the retelling of all this.

Thank you to the friends who have supported me along the way, too many to name but all loved in my heart.

It's important to know how to end something—it has to hit you just right, and it has to let go. This is what makes "St. Cloud" a perfect ending. I've heard it a thousand times, and each new time it still threatens to make me cry. A piano played slowly and carefully, a guitar gently strummed as Crutchfield's voice soars in the heavens above all things, wavering and rising to the peaks one second, and then softening slightly the next. It's the end that always gets me, when I know it's over; this is when the tears appear at the corners of my eyes. This is when I'm glad to still be here, to play it once more, lucky to be alive still and to remember all the beautiful and difficult memories of a life. Remember the love of all those we have lost, and those who are still here with us.

Burning slow, burning slow
And when I go, when I go
Look back at me, embers aglow,
When I go
When I go